Kidding Around
Las Vegas

Kidding Around
Las Vegas

A Parent's Guide
to Las Vegas

Kathy Espin

Huntington Press
Las Vegas, Nevada

Kidding Around Las Vegas
A Parent's Guide to Las Vegas

Published by
   Huntington Press
   3687 South Procyon Avenue
   Las Vegas, Nevada 89103
   Phone (702) 252-0655
   e-mail: books@huntingtonpress.com

ISBN: 0-929712-29-3

Cover Photo Credits: Desperado Roller Coaster, courtesy MGM Mirage; Las Vegas Strip, courtesy Nevada Commission on Tourism.
Cover Design: Laurie Shaw
Interior Design & Production: Laurie Shaw

Disclaimer: Although the author and publisher have made every effort to ensure the information throughout this book was accurate at press time, prices, schedules, etc., are constantly changing. Readers should always verify information before finalizing plans. The author and publisher do not assume and hereby disclaim any liability to any party for any loss or damage caused by errors or omissions, whether such errors or omissions result from negligence, accident, or any other cause.

Acknowledgments

Special thanks go to many people who helped me with this project. The first thank you goes to Anthony Curtis at Huntington Press for taking on this project and to Deke Castleman for his sage advice and precise editing. Thanks also go to Bethany Coffey, Laurie Shaw, Wendy Tucker, and Sasha Baugess at Huntington Press for all their hard work and support. Karen Silveroli of the Las Vegas Convention and Visitors Authority originally recommended me for the job of writing this book and supplied many of the photographs. My daughter and wonderful research assistant Angela Earhart gets special recognition for her valuable input. I can't forget my patient and understanding husband, Steve Baker, who supports me in everything I do. Very special thanks to all the children through whose eyes I get to see the world fresh and new over and over again. With lots of love to my granddaughters Neila, Sabrina, and Ariana Espin and to special friends Jennifer and Daniel Ciarciaglini, and Daniel McGuire.

Contents

About This Guide

Las Vegas is located in a valley in the midst of the Mojave Desert. The city itself is a very small area in the center of a metropolitan area of 1.5 million people. (The Las Vegas Strip is not in the actual city of Las Vegas. It's in the unincorporated part of the huge circumscribing Clark County.) Outside that area, there's not much. Drive in any direction from the demographic center of the metropolitan area (located somewhere around Decatur and West Charleston boulevards to the west of downtown) and, in an hour or so, you can be in the middle of desert wilderness. It's one of the things I've always loved best about living here.

The Las Vegas Strip, of course, is the heart of the metro area. It's where many residents work and it's the engine of the money machine that keeps the entire valley running. Visitors are most familiar with the area locals call the "tourist corridor," which includes the Strip (a.k.a. Las Vegas Boulevard) and downtown. This book starts with attractions found in the corridor and expands from there, taking in the valley and surrounding areas in larger and larger concentric circles. As you'll see, the farther we travel from the tourist center, the sparser the services and attractions become.

Visitors will find the handy, more popular, attractions in the early chapters of the book. Locals and out-of-towners seeking more out-of-the-way activities can focus on the latter sections.

Where possible, I've included prices so you can make budgeting decisions and hours of operation so you can budget your time, but keep in mind that these things change. By the time this book hits print, some of the activities listed here won't even exist any longer, so be sure to call ahead before heading out.

I've included activities for children of all ages and tried to indicate which age groups might get the most enjoyment out of each. If I steer you wrong, I sincerely apologize but children are unique creatures. What one 10-year-old may love, another may hate.

If your experience differs from the descriptions provided here, or if you have suggestions for attractions or experiences you think should be included in future editions of this guide, please write me in care of Huntington Press, 3687 South Procyon Avenue, Las Vegas, Nevada 89103.

Introduction

I used to be one of the few people around who would get huffy when outsiders referred to my town as "Vegas." "It's *Las* Vegas," I would snort in imitation of residents of San Francisco (not "Frisco") or San Bernardino (don't call us "San Berdoo"). Lately, I've

Welcome to Fabulous Las Vegas, courtesy Nevada Commission on Tourism

changed my mind. I've come to realize that the city I live in has a split personality and should rightfully have two names. Now, I think of "Vegas" as the place where 38 million people come to vacation every year and Las Vegas as the city that more than 1.5 million people call home. The two identities often intertwine and impact each other, but they are quite separate and distinct.

I've lived in Las Vegas for the better part of 30 years and raised three children here. We made our lives in Las Vegas, a community of homes, schools, parks, and churches much like any other, though still quite different. When I first moved here from North Carolina in 1973, it was a small town and still had a small town's heart. Everyone was from somewhere else and our newfound friends soon became family.

Today, Las Vegas is not the kind of place where neighbors bring over covered dishes when you move in or the new baby arrives. You can live next door to people for years and never know their names. Some people think the city is cold and its people hard-hearted, but I find that far from true. We make connections not through proximity, but by sharing each other's lives, work; and community activities. I made many great friends through volunteer work with the Cub Scouts, the Arthritis Foundation, United Way, the Las Vegas Civic Ballet, and others. If you look for it, the civic life is as active and fulfilling here as in any

Big Horn sheep, courtesy Nevada Commission on Tourism

city in the world. And if you want to see the heart of gold inside this flashy tart of a city, just take a look at the outpouring of love, sacrifice, and charity any time disaster strikes. Over the years we've seen many examples, such as when the MGM Grand burned in 1980 and hundreds of people rushed down to the Las Vegas Convention Center to offer aid to displaced visitors, or more recently when thousands lined up to donate blood after the 9/11 terrorist attacks.

Don't get me wrong. The "Vegas" side of the city's personality has its impact. Living in the modern equivalent of Sodom and Gomorrah certainly has its challenges. There's a crass materialism here that's hard to avoid. There's also a wide-open attitude toward sex, gambling, and alcohol that makes many people, especially parents, wince and perhaps rightfully so. And

Las Vegas Strip, courtesy Nevada Commission on Tourism

you can't completely shelter your children from it no matter how hard you try.

I think often of a story I heard many years ago. Supposedly, someone asked a father from the large Mormon community here how he reconciled his conservative faith with raising his kids in Sin City. "It's not the kids who live by the railroad tracks that get run over by the train," was the reported reply. Of course, that doesn't mean they don't play on the tracks; they're just smart enough to get out of the way when the train comes.

On the up side, the gaming industry gave me an opportunity to earn a good living that provided for my children's upbringing. It's not a bad city, but the very best of it lies just beyond the edges of the explosive development in the wide-open spaces and the small rural towns. My family has enjoyed the freedom and spirit of unbridled joy that I believe can only be found in the West. People from the Eastern Seaboard can't even imagine living where uninhabited space stretches for hundreds of miles in any direction. Las Vegas is a city, and a big one, but just outside its precincts there's room for a child to stretch his or her legs and let the heart and imagination run wild.

I'm a converted desert rat. When I first came here from North Carolina, like many others I missed the trees and grass of my native land. But over the years I've come to love the unique beauty of the desert, and I've had the privilege of introducing that wonder to many children during off-road excursions, camping trips, and day hikes. The joy of my current life is that I will be able to continue doing that for many years to come.

History of Las Vegas

Las Vegas hardly existed before the turn of the 20th century and even then there wasn't much to write home about until Hoover Dam was built in the 1930s. In the 1800s, Las Vegas (Spanish for "The Meadows") was a stop on the Old Spanish Trail that took traders back and forth from the continent's southwest interior to Los Angeles. In 1854, Mormon leader Brigham Young sent settlers from Salt Lake City to establish a colony and mine for lead in the nearby mountains. The Mormon fort built (see Old Las Vegas Mormon Fort, pg. 62) was the first non-Native American settlement in Southern Nevada, but the climate and environment were too harsh even for the hardy Mormons. In 1857, the fort was abandoned.

Although mining for gold and other valuable minerals attracted a few settlers and the State Land Act of 1885 brought a few adventurous farmers and ranchers to the area, growth was relatively stagnant until 1904, when a railroad linking Southern California and Salt Lake City established Las Vegas as a watering stop. The next year, the railroad auctioned off 700 lots in what is now downtown Las Vegas and a town was born.

In 1928, when the federal government appropriated $165 million for the construction of Hoover Dam, thousands of Depression-era job seekers began moving into the valley. Then, a few years later, Nevada Governor Fred Balzar signed the bill legalizing gambling and liberalizing divorce laws in the state. The feds, wanting to protect the dam workforce from the temptations of drinking and gambling, established Boulder City about

30 miles away to house workers. Drinking and gambling were outlawed in the government town, making Las Vegas an attractive getaway for thousands of construction workers with a little money in their pockets.

The new divorce laws also provided an economic boon to the area. A divorce could be obtained after just six weeks of residency, and soon "dude ranches" sprang up to accommodate the soon-to-be unmarried. These ranches, along with visitors traveling to see the dam, provided the beginnings of the budding tourist industry.

During World War II, the valley's isolated location (along with the water and power provided by the dam) was ideal for military and defense industries. Nellis Air Force Base was established north of town, and Basic Magnesium, Inc., was established in Henderson to provide raw materials for the nation's defense. Thousands of military and defense-industry workers temporarily swelled the area's population and many stayed after the war ended.

During the war, the tourism industry began to take off with the building of two sprawling resorts on the Los Angeles Highway, now known as the Las Vegas Strip. The El Rancho Vegas, built in 1941, was first at the corner of what is now Sahara Avenue and the Strip. The Last Frontier was built in 1942, just a couple miles to the south. Both of these properties were Western-themed, low-rise motor inns attracting auto traffic from Southern California.

About that time, a compulsive gambler named W.R. "Billy" Wilkerson decided his best chance of beating the house was to own one. But he wanted something different. Wilkerson was a successful nightclub owner from Los Angeles and the publisher of the *Hollywood Reporter*. He designed an elegant upscale resort to attract his wealthy Hollywood friends. In 1946, Wilkerson began construction on what would become the Flamingo Hotel, but his gambling problem soon got the better of his dreams. He ran out of money, opening the door for a takeover of the project by notorious gangster and murderer Ben Siegel. In fear for his life, Wilkerson, the man who many believe "dreamed up" Las Vegas, fled to Paris.

The subsequent history of the Flamingo, the city's first up-scale resort, is well documented in song and story (and a major motion picture). Siegel too ran out of money and, more impor-tantly, ran out of support from his mobster patrons. He was shot to death in 1947.

The Flamingo, however, lived on to become a landmark on the Las Vegas Strip. Not one whit of the original building re-mains, but the name lives on.

Over the next decade, more hotels sprang up, many of them fronts for organized crime. The Desert Inn opened in 1950 and the Sands and Sahara hotels in 1952. Benny Binion opened the Horseshoe Hotel downtown in 1951. In 1955, the Riviera became the first Strip high-rise at nine stories. The Hacienda, Tropicana, Stardust, and downtown's Fremont soon followed.

The 1960s saw the advent of the corporate takeover of the casino business. Howard Hughes started the trend when he moved into the penthouse suites at the Desert Inn. Legend has it that hotel management asked Hughes and company to va-cate the suites so they could accommodate incoming high roll-ers. Hughes replied by buying the hotel. The purchase kicked off a buying spree the likes of which the city has never seen since. Between 1966 and 1968, Hughes bought the Desert Inn, Sands, Castaways, New Frontier, and Silver Slipper on the Las Vegas Strip, and the Landmark just off the Strip. Of those, only the Frontier still stands today. The Desert Inn and Sands were sold to Kirk Kerkorian, who went on to build not one, but two, MGM Grand hotels. Steve Wynn eventually bought the Castaways and tore it down to build the Mirage. He recently imploded most of the Desert Inn to make way for his newest megaresort, Wynn Las Vegas.

Hughes' impact on the gaming industry was only the tip of the iceberg. In the 1950s, Hughes bought 22,500 acres of land on the western edge of the valley and in 1985, almost a decade after the billionaire's death in 1976, the Howard Hughes Corporation announced it would build a planned community of homes and businesses on what was then called Hughes Site. Today, the development is called Summerlin and is home to more than 67,000 people. The company says more than 160,000 will call Summerlin home by the time the project is completed in 2020.

The growth of the casino-resort industry began a population boom that has never stopped. In 1960, the city had a population of just over 64,000 and the county was home to 127,000. By 1980, the county population had bloomed to 463,000, and today the valley is home to 1.5 million people, with an estimated 5,000 people moving in every month.

Corporate America and public trading of casino stock has been good to the Las Vegas gaming industry. In the last 20 years, an unprecedented building boom has added more than 60,000 hotel rooms and dozens of major resorts to the Las Vegas Strip.

Today Las Vegas is one of the fastest growing cities in the country, outpaced only by its bedroom communities of Henderson and North Las Vegas. Many visitors are surprised to find a thriving residential community existing just beyond the glare of the neon of the tourist corridor. Of course, we are a little different in some ways. Not many cities have slot machines in the grocery stores.

Children and Gaming

Las Vegas runs on gambling, alcohol, and sex. These are not family-friendly activities. Local laws strictly prohibit children from loitering in gaming areas and near slot machines wherever they are located. Children (anyone under 21) aren't even allowed to stand around and watch while their parents gamble. Children are allowed to pass through casino areas on their way to restaurants or other attractions, but are not allowed to stop and hang out. Although many parents find it inconvenient, it's the law and if security staff at your hotel seems unreasonably strict, it's for good reason. The casino can lose its valuable gaming license or face stiff fines for letting children loiter in gaming areas.

Getting Around

Las Vegas might be one of the easiest cities in the world to drive around in. Traffic, except on the Strip, is relatively light and visibility is good. Streets are laid out in a straightforward grid and very few (most of them downtown) go only one way. Major east/west streets crossing the Strip are named for the hotels they pass. An added bonus is the lack of hills and trees. The hotels make excellent landmarks that can be seen for miles in all directions. The streets are wide and the traffic lights are timed.

Locals like to complain about the traffic and the rudeness of drivers, but it makes me wonder how a city with so many new residents can have so many people who are naïve about relative conditions. Compared to other cities, we have *no* traffic and, except for our ever-rushing cabbies, drivers are as courteous as anywhere, except maybe in the tourist areas where alcohol tends to fog brains.

The Strip gets clogged almost nightly. Strip traffic creeps on weekends and comes to a halt on major holidays. On New Year's Eve, for example, the street is closed down completely to make room for hoards of revelers. This celebration is no place for children and I even wonder about the sanity of the adults who attend.

Parking is free and plentiful almost everywhere you go, except in the downtown area. Even there, the hotels offer some free parking; however, parking on the streets is metered and most parking spaces are found in municipal parking garages. The Strip hotels offer free valet parking, but it is customary to tip the valet parker a dollar or two when your car is returned.

Walking in the tourist areas may be more dangerous than driving. We lose several visitors each year who insist on jaywalking. Pedestrian overpasses are provided at the major Strip intersections and others have lights and crossing areas. The wise visitor uses them and still looks both ways.

Public transportation is plentiful on the Strip and around downtown. The Citizens Area Transit (CAT) bus system moves up and down the Strip and covers downtown. Trolleys run from the Stratosphere to Mandalay Bay for $1.75 per ride and are great for casino hopping. Taxis are available outside every resort and are convenient but, of course, expensive.

A recently opened monorail system runs from the MGM Grand to the Sahara on the east side of the Strip. The trains stop at several resorts along the way and at the Las Vegas Convention Center. Rides are $3 each way with discounts for round trip and day passes.

Public transportation for the rest of the valley is available, but slow and complicated. Taxis will begrudgingly take you to locations outside the tourist corridor, but it's difficult to get them to come back and pick you up. And, finally, although many of the local casinos provide shuttle service to the Strip, a rental car is recommended for getting around the valley.

Play it Safe

A few safety precautions should be exercised. The crime rate in Las Vegas is relatively high, especially on the edges of downtown. For safety, valet parking is recommended at night and in the daytime in some of the rougher sections, such as at the northern end of the Strip between Sahara Avenue and Fremont Street downtown. Be sure to avoid dark isolated parking areas and always be aware of your surroundings. Most hotels will provide a security escort to the parking lot if you ask.

The summer heat provides another threat to health and safety. Temperatures climb to well above 100 degrees for several weeks and often go higher than 110 degrees. I don't care what they say about dry heat, 112 degrees is miserable no matter what the humidity.

Relentless sun and furnace-like winds take their toll. Be sure to drink plenty of water and make sure your children do too. Drink before you get thirsty and consider a sports drink occasionally to replace salt and electrolytes. You might not sweat in the Las Vegas heat, but that doesn't mean you aren't losing moisture; it just means the sweat is drying up faster than you can produce it.

The distance between hotels is deceiving. The buildings are so huge they look much closer than they are. From the Flamingo, for example, it looks like Caesars Palace is just across the street, but it's a considerable hike from the Flamingo's front door till you reach air conditioning at Caesars. Consider taking a taxi, bus, or monorail even for what appear to be short trips, especially for the short-legged set.

For any outdoor activity, summer or winter, be sure to use a good sunscreen, and a hat is a must. The lack of humidity means the sun is especially bright. It'll skin your hide in a wink.

Hiking, camping, and other outdoor activities should be limited when the weather is really hot and, even in milder times, be sure to take along plenty of water. A gallon per person per day in the desert is recommended.

With all this talk about sun, heat, and lack of humidity, it seems funny to have to mention the other hazard of the Las Vegas desert: flash flooding. The desert floor doesn't do a very good job of soaking up water so, when it does rain, there's a tendency to flood. Water can suddenly come crashing down from the surrounding mountains as it makes its way across the valley to Lake Mead. Don't ever cross water running in the street unless you're sure of the depth (as in, you've seen some fool ford the pool before you). Don't let children play in floodwater during a storm and do not go around barricades put up by law enforcement.

In the rain, Las Vegas streets become especially slick. The oil and tire residue that builds up on the streets rises to the top of the water, creating perfect conditions for hydroplaning. Slow down and keep plenty of room between you and the car in front of you.

The desert is a wonderful place to live and to play, but common sense and awareness can avert disaster.

Make Time to Relax

I've listed lots of things for visitors to do here in Las Vegas, but whatever you do, try not to do too much. Make time to relax and enjoy your time off with your children. Your hotel pool is a great place to have fun. Perhaps arrange your day so you're back at your hotel for an afternoon rest period. If your kids are too old for a nap, play a board game in the hotel room or watch a movie on the in-room TV.

Pace yourselves and enjoy our city. You'll find there's no place quite like it in the world.

The Tourist Corridor

Welcome to the Adult Disneyland. While the Las Vegas Strip and Downtown are known for the pleasures offered adults, there are lots of activities for families too. If you choose wisely, you can spend an entire vacation enjoying wholesome entertainment. Warning: You won't be able to entirely avoid drunken gamblers and semi-nude women, but there are enough distractions to keep the kids from asking too many awkward questions.

See It for Free

Many Las Vegas resorts have developed free attractions as loss-leaders to attract visitors in hopes they will spend some money while they are there. In the case of downtown Las Vegas, the hotels have combined resources to provide one huge attraction. Since you'll have children with you, you won't be tempted to play, so you can take advantage of the freebies without paying the price. This is the only sure way to win in Las Vegas.

You could spend an entire vacation just checking out the free stuff but you will probably find it more enjoyable to combine the freebies with other attractions as some of the sights are hardly worth a trip in themselves.

Attractions are arranged from north to south with two off-Strip attractions at the end.

Fremont Street Experience, courtesy Fremont Street Experience (right) and Nevada Commission on Tourism (below)

Fremont Street Experience

Downtown Las Vegas
Fremont Street between Main Street and Las Vegas Boulevard
800-249-3559
www.vegasexperience.com
Hours: Shows hourly from 7 p.m. to midnight nightly.
Directions and Parking: Drive one block north of Fremont Street on Las Vegas Boulevard to Ogden Street. A public parking lot is located at Las Vegas Boulevard and Ogden.

The idea is simple but the effect is stunning. A huge LED display of 12 million lights has been made into a five-block canopy over an outdoor pavilion. The pavilion connects the old hotels located in downtown Las Vegas. Free light and music shows are seen hourly in the evenings. The shows include "Area 51," a tribute to the legendary secret base north of Las Vegas (see write-up on Rachel, pgs. 137-140); "The Drop," a mythical underwater journey; and "American Freedom," a tribute to all things patriotic. The pavilion (declared a city park so it would qualify for city funds) becomes party central for holidays and special events like the National Finals Rodeo in December.

At the east end of the pavilion is Neonopolis, a retail and entertainment center that houses restaurants, a movie theater, an arcade, and various shops. It can make a nice refuge for families that don't want to take their children into the nearby casinos for restroom breaks and snacks.

Downtown is the Las Vegas center for the homeless. Some less-than-savory characters can be seen loitering about at all hours. Law enforcement works hard at keeping the area safe and respectable, but it's an uphill battle that pits the rights of the down-and-out against the needs of the tourists and business owners in the area. Be prepared for some "colorful" sights and I don't just mean the light show.

Neon Museum

Fremont Street at Las Vegas Boulevard and Third Street
702/387-6366
www.neonmuseum.org
Hours: 24 hours, seven days a week.
Directions and Parking: Drive one block north of Fremont Street on Las Vegas Boulevard to Ogden Street. A public parking lot is located at Las Vegas Boulevard and Ogden.

Where else in the world would you find an outdoor public museum dedicated to antique neon signs? The Neon Museum officially began in 1996 when the horse and rider sign from the old Hacienda Hotel was restored and installed at the corner of Las Vegas Boulevard and Fremont Street, just outside of Neonopolis. Today, the museum consists of a second outdoor site at the Third Street cul-de-sac adjacent to the Fremont Street Experience canopy. Among the museum's 10 signs are a genie's lamp from the original Aladdin Hotel and a very old Chief Hotel sign from a motel located on East Fremont Street in the '40s.

The museum foundation owns an outdoor "boneyard" of pieces in various stages of restoration, but the facility is no longer open to the public. Guided tours of the Neon Museum are available for groups of 10 or more. The guided tours are $5 for adults and $3 for students first grade through college (with ID) and seniors 60 and over. Children five and under are free.

Circus Acts

Circus Circus Hotel and Casino
2880 Las Vegas Boulevard South
702/734-0410
www.circuscircus.com
Hours: Daily, 11 a.m. to midnight.
Parking: Convenient self-parking is available at the rear of the building.

We locals owe Circus Circus a debt of gratitude for keeping out-of-work curtain acts off the welfare rolls by employing them in the casino. This loss-leader is known as the "World's Largest Permanent Circus"; but then, how many permanent circuses do you know of? The Midway Stage on the second floor over the main casino at Circus Circus features live free circus acts every 30 minutes. You won't see anything here that you haven't seen before, but the kids will enjoy it and the price is right. Acts include jugglers, clowns, contortionists, trapeze artists, aerialists, and trained dogs. A live (though the musicians' lack of enthusiasm makes you wonder sometimes) three-piece combo provides music. Warning: You can easily spend $20 or more per child on the carnival games while waiting for the show to begin.

Sirens of TI

> TI (a.k.a. Treasure Island)
> 3300 Las Vegas Boulevard South
> 702/894-7111
> 800-288-7206
> www.treasureislandlasvegas.com
> Hours: Dusk to 11:30 p.m. or so. Times vary with the season.
> Parking: Easiest access is to park in valet parking at the Spring
> Mountain Road entrance. The public parking lot is behind the
> hotel.

The Las Vegas Strip frontage of the TI, formerly known as Treasure Island, has been made into an elaborate pirate's village on a man-made bay. There used to be a great family show with pirate battles and sinking ships but the hotel has decided to target a more adult market and has changed the show (note the risqué photo below). Now they have added sex to the good old-fashioned violence. In the show, mythical sirens lure a pirate ship to its doom, then the survivors board the sirens' ship for an all-out party. The show includes some swashbuckling and pyrotechnics and a long (overlong, some say) rock-and-roll after-party.

Sirens of TI, courtesy TI

Mirage volcano (top),
courtesy MGM Mirage

The Mirage Lobby (center),
courtesy MGM Mirage

Mirage Tiger Habitat (left),
courtesy MGM Mirage

Younger children won't get the plot of this thing at all; it's so convoluted even the adults don't always get it. But hey, it's free, the ships are interesting, and the stunts are fun.

The show can be seen every 90 minutes, weather permitting. Crowds gather quickly for every performance. Viewing areas have been created on a wooden walkway that runs in front of the bay. Because the show creates the perfect distraction, the area is a favorite with pickpockets. Be sure to watch your wallet as well as your kids.

If you don't mind spending a few bucks, the Buccaneer Bay Club restaurant inside the hotel offers Continental cuisine with a view of the show. The restaurant is pricey. A recent Zagat survey listed the average meal at $49; nevertheless, some folks say the show is better than the food.

Be sure to call for show times.

Mirage Volcano, Aquarium, and Tiger Habitat

Mirage
3400 Las Vegas Boulevard South
702/791-7111
www.themirage.com
Volcano Hours: Every 15 minutes from 6 p.m. to midnight.
Parking: Park in valet parking off Las Vegas Boulevard.

A clever combination of water, light, fire, and sound effects nicely recreates the explosion and lava flow of a volcano erupting nightly in front of the Mirage. With all the other socko-wow-ie attractions on the Strip, the enthusiasm for this one has faded over the years, but it's still fun to see simulated fire spew 100 feet into the air. The best spot for viewing is the second-floor Outback Steakhouse across the street at the Casino Royale. It reminds me of the "Restaurant at the End of the Universe" from Douglas Adams' "Hitchhiker's Guide to the Galaxy," where a time machine plays the end of time over and over again for the amusement of the diners. The volcano doesn't compare with cosmic implosion but it still makes interesting dinner entertainment.

Mirage Aquarium
Hours: 24 hours.
Parking: Valet park at the south entrance off Spring Mountain Road.

Behind the Mirage's front desk is a 20,000-gallon saltwater aquarium, home to angelfish, puffer fish, tangs, sharks, and other exotic sea creatures. The aquarium accommodates more than 1,000 coral-reef animals representing 60 species from Australia, Hawaii, Tonga, Fiji, the Red Sea, the Marshall Islands, the Sea of Cortez, and the Caribbean. Billed as "one of the most elaborate and technically advanced aquariums in the world," the tank is 53 feet long, eight feet tall, and six feet deep. The seascape is a simulated coral reef.

White Tiger Habitat
Hours: Open 24 hours.

Located in a shopping promenade south of the Mirage lobby area is the Royal White Tiger Habitat, where some of Siegfried and Roy's tigers lounge occasionally for the enjoyment of passersby. There might be three to four tigers on display at any one time as the animals are rotated between the habitat and Siegfried and Roy's private enclave. The display is designed to replicate the snowy Himalayan Mountain habitat the tigers would naturally call home. The tigers even have their own pool and fountains to play in, but the animals don't do much because, well, that's what tigers do. Like most domesticated cats that don't have to hunt for their food, they lounge around a lot. Still, they're a spectacular sight to see.

Flamingo Wildlife Habitat

Flamingo Las Vegas
3555 Las Vegas Boulevard South
702/733-3111
800-732-2111
www.caesars.com
Hours: Penguin feeding 8:30 a.m. and 3 p.m.
Parking: Park in valet parking or in the parking garage, both on the south side of the hotel.

The Flamingo Las Vegas has transformed its pool area into a 15-acre tropical paradise with flower gardens, fountains, pools, waterfalls, and streams. Located in this area is a wildlife habitat housing swans, Mandarin ducks, parrots, koi fish, turtles, and other rare and common species. Surprisingly, the collection also includes African penguins and, not so surprisingly, Chilean flamingos. The penguins are the big attraction.

People often associate penguins with cold climates and are quite shocked to see the animals living in the Las Vegas heat. Keep in mind: These African penguins are quite happy in the heat. They do have a problem with the lack of humidity, but misters keep them moist and healthy. The Flamingo is part of a Species Survival Program and is breeding the African penguins to help maintain a strong population. The penguins are fed at 8:30 a.m. and 3 p.m. daily, which is a show in itself. The

Flamingos, courtesy Park Place Entertainment

garden and habitat are visible from the Flamingo's buffet, making for an inexpensive lunch- or dinner-and-show opportunity.

Forum Shops at Caesars

Caesars Palace
3500 Las Vegas Boulevard South
702/893-4800
www.simon.com
Hours: Animatronic statue show every hour on the hour, 10 a.m. to 11 p.m. weekdays and until midnight on weekends. Atlantis Aquarium feedings, Monday through Friday, 1:15 and 5:15 p.m. Aquarium tour, Monday through Friday, 3:15 p.m.
Parking: Park in the garage in back of the resort accessible from the drive on the north side of the hotel. Take the elevator to the casino. Walk into the casino and look ahead to the left; the Forum Shops are just across the casino.

Listing this attraction under things to do for free is a bit misleading. Be forewarned; take this trip with your spending limits

Forum Fountain, courtesy Park Place Entertainment

firmly established. You can spend the kids' college tuition here in the blink of an eye. The free part is the mall itself. Designed to resemble an ancient Roman market plaza, the domed ceiling is painted to look like the sky with lighting that progresses from sunrise to dusk in the course of an hour. The two rotundas in the mall feature animatronic Roman statuaries.

In the Fountain Festival in the center of the main mall area, Bacchus and a crew of partiers including Plutus, Venus, and Apollo come to life hourly and sing and move around in a seven-minute show that includes music, lasers, and lighting effects. In the *Lost City of Atlantis* show in the Great Roman Hall, an animatronic Neptune and his feuding kids do battle with lasers, fire, and steam around a 50,000 gallon salt-water aquarium with 500 tropical fish. A scuba diver feeds the fish at 3:15 and 7:15 p.m., which makes an interesting show in itself. A free behind-the-scenes tour of the Atlantis Aquarium, hosted by a marine biologist and a scuba-diving aquarist, gives a close-up view of the aquarium and its workings. Tour times are subject to change, so be sure to call ahead.

Bellagio Fountains

Bellagio
3600 Las Vegas Boulevard South
702/693-7111
www.bellagiolasvegas.com
Hours: Vary with the seasons.
Parking: Closest parking is valet at the Flamingo Road entrance. Self-parking is on the south side of the building, a long hike to the fountains.

In front of Bellagio is a nine-acre lake sporting 1,200 individually controlled fountain jets that shoot as high as 240 feet in the air. Every half-hour during the day and every 15 minutes at night the fountains perform a computer-controlled ballet of light, water, and music. Musical selections include classic Italian opera and popular hits from singers such as Frank Sinatra (a personal friend of Steve Wynn, the gaming magnate who built the hotel). The idea is simple, downright trite, but the total effect is spectacular.

Viewing is best from the sidewalk in front of the hotel, but the show can also be seen from the pedestrian overpass that runs over the Las Vegas Strip. Again, keep one eye on your wallet and one on your kids.

Bellagio Fountains, courtesy MGM Mirage

Bellagio Conservatory

Hours: 24 hours.
Parking: Park in the garage to the south of the hotel. The conservatory is right next to the garage.

Bellagio's botanical garden is grand and lovely. The displays change with the season and smell as wonderful as they look. All the horticulture is live and fresh, grown in a huge greenhouse in back of the hotel.

M&M's World

Showcase Mall
3785 Las Vegas Boulevard South
702/597-3122
www.mms.com
Hours: Sunday through Thursday, 9 a.m. to 6 p.m,; Friday and Saturday, 9 a.m. to 8 p.m.
Parking: There is a parking garage behind the Showcase Mall.

The window-shopping is great and it's free if you can resist 26,000 square feet of retail space offering everything you can think of with an M&M logo on it. You can see the famous M&M spokescandies on a movie set where you can take a photo with your favor-

M&M World, courtesy M&M Mars Corp.

ite character. The M&M Academy is on the third floor. There, a wacky professor takes patrons on a tour of the M&M classroom and through an off-the-wall set of exhibits. A highlight of the tour is the Colorworks with 24 different M&M colors, some you've never dreamed of and some you would never want to (could you bring yourself to eat a gray M&M?). The tour ends with a 3D movie about Red and Yellow's trip to Las Vegas. The tour ends with a surprise treat.

Lion Habitat

MGM Grand
3799 Las Vegas Boulevard South
702/891-1111
www.mgmgrand.com
Hours: Daily, 11 a.m. to 10 p.m.
Parking: There is no good place to park at the MGM. Park in valet on Tropicana and still plan to take a hike to the habitat

MGM Grand Lion Habitat, courtesy MGM Mirage

located near the Las Vegas Strip entrance to the hotel. Free parking is available in the huge garage behind the hotel.

The famous MGM mascot, the lion, has been honored with a special habitat and exhibit space inside the MGM Grand Casino just a short walk from the Tropicana/Las Vegas Boulevard entrance. The hotel says the 5,345-square-foot facility cost about $9 million to build in 1999. The habitat is built in three levels with a glass observation tunnel running through it. There are artificial rocks and cliffs for the lions to play and rest on and a waterfall. Trainers enter a large enclosure to play with the animals for the viewer's enjoyment. While going through the glass tunnel, visitors can safely get up close with these magnificent animals. They can be over, under, or around you at any time.

Usually, three lions are in residence at any one time. The lions are rotated daily from the habitat to the nearby ranch of owner and trainer Keith Evans. They're washed and examined by a vet before being transported back to the habitat.

The habitat has formed an alliance with the Minnesota Lions Research Center. There is a gift shop providing stuffed lions, plastic lions, glass lions and all manner of lion T-shirts, jackets, and so on, that you can't miss if you try (the exit goes right through the shop). A portion of the proceeds from the gift shop goes to the research center.

The shift change for the lions takes place daily between 3:30 and 4:30 p.m.; only one or two lions are visible when the animals are changed out.

Warn the kids that lions don't do much, even in their natural habitat. Sleeping and hanging out is pretty much the extent of it. Handlers go in often to attempt to get the lions to play, but it's a tough sell. You can see them jump over the glass tunnel sometimes but that's about as exciting as it gets. A recorded roar is played often, and the kids think it's the real thing.

Tropicana Bird Show and Air Play

Tropicana Hotel and Casino
3801 Las Vegas Boulevard South
702/739-2222
www.tropicanalv.com
Hours: 11 a.m., 12:30 p.m., and 2 p.m. daily except Thursday.
Parking: Use valet parking on Las Vegas Boulevard.

Tropicana Bird Show, courtesy Tropicana Hotel and Casino

Tropicana Air Play, courtesy Tropicana Hotel and Casino

Trainer Tiana Carroll's talented and amazing birds perform in the Tropics Lounge. A green-winged macaw is the comic in the act. She follows Tiana around and cuts up for the audience. A Moluccan cockatoo talks, rides a motorcycle, and even roller blades. A yellow-nape Amazon parrot and a Congo-African parrot sing "How Much is That Doggie in the Window" in duet. Audience members are encouraged to participate in the show and the person who cheers the loudest gets his or her picture taken with Tiana and one of the birds.

Air Play
Hours: Daily, 3, 5, 7:30, and 9:30 p.m.

On your way to see the Bird Show, you might get lucky and see *Air Play*. Acrobats, aerialists, jugglers, and other modern circus acts perform right above the casino floor on top of slot machines and in the air under the casino's famous 4,000-square-foot stained-glass dome. Children are not allowed to loiter on the casino floor, but the show takes place right inside the casino's front entrance so you might be able to watch from a distance.

Rock 'n' Roll Collection
Hard Rock Hotel and Casino
4455 Paradise Road
702/693-5000
www.hardrockhotel.com
Hours: Open 24 hours.
Directions: East from the Strip on Harmon Avenue
Parking: Valet parking is on the south side of the building. A large garage is on the north.

Tell the kids this is the hotel where the Who's John Entwhistle died so they can say "Who?" The hotel is the logical offshoot of the famous chain of rock 'n' roll-themed restaurants and houses an impressive collection of memorabilia. Artifacts are scattered throughout the hotel but most of the displays can be seen on the promenade surrounding the circular casino. The collection, valued at $2 million, includes guitars from Nirvana, ZZ Top, Pearl Jam, Van Halen, and Bruce Springsteen. Tons of costumes are on display including outfits worn by the Red Hot Chili Peppers and Madonna, along with Elvis' gold lamé jacket. You can see gold and platinum records from David Bowie, the Beatles, and Billy Joel, as well as Elton John's rhinestone-covered piano and The Doors' John Densmore's drums. A Hard Rock Café sits on the corner in front of the hotel.

The folks at the Hard Rock were quite adamant about not being included in this book. Families with children are not part of their market demographic, you see. Security there may be a bit more strident about enforcing the "No Kids" rule.

Sunset Stampede

Sam's Town Hotel and Gambling Hall
5111 Boulder Highway
702/456-7777
www.samstownlv.com
Hours: Shows are at 2, 6, 8, and 10 p.m. daily.
Directions: From the Las Vegas Strip, take Flamingo Road east to Boulder Highway. Sam's Town is on your right.
Parking: Park on the third floor of the parking garage off Flamingo Road.

Mystic Park, courtesy Sam's Town Hotel and Gambling Hall

Mystic Falls Park at Sam's Town (they prefer to call it an indoor park rather than an atrium) is a cool oasis of trees, plants, falls, and streams plus animatronic animals. In this faux forest, a beaver builds a dam, an owl hoots overhead, and squirrels gambol. Four times a day a wolf howls and emerges from his den to mark the beginning of a water-and-laser show that chronicles the pioneers' journey across the prairie. The lights and fountains dance to music from the "Grand Canyon Suite" recorded by the Indianapolis Philharmonic Orchestra. The show is free and so is the stroll through the park. There are no slot machines or gaming tables in the park, so children are welcome.

Masquerade Show in the Sky

Rio All-Suite Hotel and Casino
3700 West Flamingo Road
702/777-7777
www.harrahs.com
Hours: Shows are at 3, 4, 5, 6:30, 7:30, 8:30, and 9:30 p.m. daily.
Directions: From Las Vegas Boulevard, take Flamingo Road west. The Rio is on the right.
Parking: For easy access, park in the garage on the east side of the hotel.

In this upbeat 15-minute show, huge lighted parade floats circle the ceiling of the slot area on the south end of the casino, while a cast of 15 or so dancers take to a stage below. Dancers on the floats throw Mardi Gras beads to the audience standing below and on second floor balconies surrounding the area. The theme, of course, is Carnival, so the music is lively and the costumes colorful. Just so you know, Rio management didn't really want to promote the *Show in the Sky* to families. They say they recently revamped the show and made it sexier to discourage parents from bringing their children. The ploy didn't really work. The show isn't all that sexy compared to what your children see on TV every day. Because the show takes place in a gaming area, children are not encouraged to watch from the floor. However, they're allowed to watch from the balconies. The show is free, but for $9.95 you can purchase a ticket to ride in the parade in the sky. Children are allowed to participate as long as they're 32 inches or taller. Purchase tickets at the box office.

Masquerade Show in the Sky, courtesy Harrah's Entertainment

Not So Free, But Fun to See

Now that we've covered the free stuff, we'll move on to the attractions you must pay to see. They range from the reasonably priced, at a few bucks per person, to the outrageous. They are arranged by type of attraction and then by location from north to south. Try combining some of the free attractions with one special pay-to-see treat.

Lions, Tigers, and Sharks, Oh My!

Siegfried & Roy's Secret Garden and Dolphin Habitat

Mirage

3400 Las Vegas Boulevard South

702/791-7111

www.themirage.com

Hours: Generally from 11 a.m. to 5 p.m.; vary seasonally and for major holidays.

Parking: Park in valet parking on the north side of the building off Spring Mountain Road.

This mini-zoo is done up with Las Vegas pizzazz. Animals featured here include three breeds of tigers, a panther, a snow leopard, and an Asian elephant. A combination of fake and real vegetation simulates a jungle atmosphere. An audio tour by Siegfried gives lots of background on the animals and their habitats, plus a good bit of razzmatazz about how Siegfried, Roy, and the Mirage are dedicated to saving the animals from extinction.

Dolphin Habitat, courtesy MGM Mirage

The Secret Garden alone would not be worth the price of admission ($10, children under 10 free) if not combined with the Dolphin Habitat, home to eight Atlantic bottlenose dolphins. On Wednesdays, when the Secret Garden is closed, viewing the habitat alone is half price. The display is billed as a research habitat. Some of the dolphins do tricks, but the hotel claims they're not trained. The habitat includes a 22-foot-deep viewing tank that can be seen from above or from an underground viewing area. The births of several dolphins born in the habitat can be seen on video. The 2.5-million-gallon facility is often toured by local school kids escorted by marine biologists.

Shark Reef and Aquarium

Mandalay Bay
3950 Las Vegas Boulevard South
702/632-7777
www.mandalaybay.com
Hours: Daily, 10 a.m. to 11 p.m.
Parking: Self and valet parking are available in the back of the hotel at the event center's entrance.

If your kids are into fish and sharks, you really can't miss this attraction. Around 2,000 animals from 75 different species can be seen in this extensive display. From a 12-foot-long nurse shark to a one-inch guppy, you can see it all. There are angelfish, tang fish, and puffer fish; crocodiles, sea turtles, and Moray eels; reef sharks, lemon sharks, and too many more to name. You might even catch the scuba-diving aquarists during their daily maintenance dive. One of my favorite features is the Plexiglas tunnel that allows you to walk through the aquarium. Another is a huge glass cylinder filled with jellyfish lit with a black light. It looks like something from a sci-fi movie. A recorded self-guided tour is available. Although little ones love this exhibit, older children will get more out of it. Admission is $14.95 for adults and $9.95 for children five to 12. Children under five are free. Nevada residents receive a $3 discount on all tickets.

Mandalay Bay Aquarium
Hours: 24 hours.

While you're at Mandalay Bay, stop by to see the aquarium. Located in the main lobby, the 12,000-gallon saltwater aquarium stands two stories high. The aquarium is home to several species of tropical fish, including soldier fish, angelfish, and Pacific black-tip sharks. It's a close second to the Mirage Aquarium previously mentioned.

Shark Reef Tunnel (above), courtesy Mandalay Bay Corp.

Mandalay Bay Aquarium (right), courtesy Mandalay Bay Corp.

Not Your Daddy's Museum

What kind of museum would you expect to see in Las Vegas? Gambling Hall of Fame? Showgirl Museum? Got 'em. Freak shows? Elvis collections? Got those too. The selection can range from collections of classic art to collections of classic cars. Below are some collections children from small to large might enjoy. Again, they are arranged geographically from north to south along the tourist corridor.

Star Trek: The Experience

Las Vegas Hilton
3000 Paradise Road
702/732-5111
www.startrekexp.com
Hours: Sunday through Thursday, 11 a.m. to 10 p.m.; Friday and Saturday, 11 a.m. to 11 p.m.
Parking: Convenient access from the parking garage on the north side of the building.

This is the Star Trek fan's nirvana. Star Trek: The Experience is an interactive adventure that brings the Starship Enterprise and the characters of its offspring to life. You might even get to

Entrance (left), courtesy Star Trek: The Experience

USS Enterprise bridge (facing page), courtesy Star Trek: The Experience

meet a Klingon or a Ferengi in person. I had the privilege of meeting both, and it wasn't as unpleasant as you might think. The attraction comes in three parts. First is the History of the Future self-guided exhibit that leads to the motion-simulator rides. It's arranged in a time line that incorporates the plots of every Star Trek TV show and movie ever made. The display includes 200 costumes, weapons, special effects, and props used in the shows. There's way more here than the average child will have patience for. They will be much more interested in heading straight for the rides at the end of the exhibit walkway.

There are now two rides. In the "Klingon Encounter," you get "beamed up" to the transporter room of the USS Enterprise (a personal fantasy of mine), have a briefing on the bridge, then take a Turbolift to board a shuttlecraft for a four-minute mission to do battle with the bad guys. There's a fun surprise ending to look out for, but I won't spoil it for you.

In the BORG Invasion 4D, visitors are attacked by the evil BORG, and go through a simulated assimilation (try to say that fast three times). All the senses are involved for an eerily realistic adventure.

The Experience is expensive in my opinion. For a tour of the museum and both rides, admission is $34.99 per person and

$31.99 for children under 12 and seniors over 65. Admission for either the BORG Invasion or Klingon Encounter is $29.99 per person and $26.99 for children under 12 and seniors over 65. (Nevada residents receive a $5 discount.) That means, at minimum, a family of four will drop more than a hundred bucks before even thinking about souvenirs from the shops on the Deep Space Nine Promenade or lunch at Quark's Bar and Restaurant. Is it worth it? Depends on just how big a Star Trek nut you are.

By the way, children must be taller than 42 inches to enter.

Elvis-A-Rama

3401 Industrial Road
702/309-7200
www.elvisarama.com
Hours: Daily, 10 a.m. to 6 p.m.
Directions: Heading north on Las Vegas Boulevard, turn left on Stardust Lane. On Industrial Road, turn right.
Parking: There is a large parking lot at the front door and rarely much business.

Come now, would it really be Vegas without an Elvis museum? Management claims this is the largest collection of

Elvis-A-Rama, courtesy
Elvis-A-Rama

Elvis-related items outside of Graceland. The collection includes clothes, jewelry, costumes, cars, and even the King's personal speedboat. There's also a gift shop (who'd have thought?). Fortunately, this venue employs at least three or four Elvis "tribute" acts at any one time. With so many in town, it's nice to see some of them get regular work. The entry fee for the museum is $9.95 with children under 12 free. Shows run from $14.95 to $19.95. Packages including a show and the museum tour run from $22 to $27. This place is a must for the die-hard Elvis fan, but if your child is among them, I suggest you have a really strange kid there.

Madame Tussaud's Celebrity Encounter
Venetian
3355 Las Vegas Boulevard South
702/414-4500
www.madame-tussauds.com
Hours: Summer, 10 a.m. to 11 p.m. daily. Hours change with the season.
Parking: Park in the garage on the south side of the Venetian.

Where else can you come face to face with stars such as Frank Sinatra, Muhammad Ali, Elvis Presley, Tiger Woods, Jennifer Lopez, Ben Affleck, and Wayne Newton all in one place? The Las Vegas version of the famous London wax works offers replicas of more than 100 celebrities. Visitors are invited behind the scenes to see how the intricate replicas are created. Sculptors take more than 150 precise measurements of the subject and spend more than six months making sure the wax statue is exact. This exhibit focuses on United States icons and even hosts a "Spirit of America" exhibit that includes George Washington, Abraham Lincoln, and John and Jackie Kennedy. The museum is expensive. General admission is $20.95 for adults, $14.95 for seniors 60 and older and students over 12, $9.95 for children six to 12, and children under five are free. Audio wands can be rented for an additional $3, though they're not necessary to enjoy the exhibit. Don't forget your camera. Older kids will especially enjoy having photos taken with their idols.

NASCAR Café

> Sahara Hotel and Casino
> 2535 Las Vegas Boulevard South
> 702/734-7223
> www.nascarcafelasvegas.com
> Hours: Monday through Thursday, 11 a.m. to
> 10 p.m.; Friday, 11 a.m. to 11 p.m.; Saturday, 10 a.m. to midnight; and Sunday, 9 a.m. to 10 p.m.
> Parking: Park in valet or in the parking garage in the rear of the hotel off Paradise Road.

This is the place for NASCAR fans. The themed restaurant often hosts autograph sessions with NASCAR drivers during the big race in March. All the NASCAR races, driver profiles, and NASCAR news can be seen on giant TV screens with surround sound. Bill Frances Boulevard runs through the lower level of the café and features NASCAR memorabilia, including Nextel Cup cars. The world's largest stock car, "Carzilla," serves as the centerpiece of the Carzilla Bar. The menu in the restaurant is strictly all-American and a bit pricey, though not as bad as some. Sandwiches run $6.95 to $8.50 and entrées from $7.95 to $16.95.

Auto Collections

> Imperial Palace Hotel and Casino
> 3535 Las Vegas Boulevard South
> 702/794-3174
> www.AutoCollections.com

Hours: Daily, 9:30 a.m. to 9:30 p.m.
Parking: Park in the parking garage and take the elevator to the fifth floor.

I haven't yet met a teenage boy (or many girls) who didn't like cars. The Imperial Palace Auto Collections are car heaven. Even folks who aren't car nuts enjoy this museum. Here you have more than 300 classic cars valued at between $20,000 and $1.5 million each. The collection includes race cars, muscle cars, touring roadsters, and more. Highlights include a 1933 Duesenberg Roadster, one of the 1967 Ford Mustangs known as "Eleanor" in the movie *Gone in Sixty Seconds*, and an 1886 Benz three-wheeler. This isn't just a museum, it's a classic car emporium where cars are bought and sold. The collection also includes rare factory and one-of-a-kind models and houses a Franklin Mint store. A gift shop offers automotive signs, gas-pump lamps, books, and collectibles. The collection is located on the fifth floor of the hotel parking garage. Admission is $6.95 for adults, $3 for seniors 65 and older and children 12 and under. Good deal for the price but even better for free. You can often find staffers handing out free coupons in and outside of

Imperial Palace Auto Collections, courtesy Imperial Palace Hotel and Casino

the casino. A security guard in the elevator had a pocketful of them on a recent trip. Coupons are also in the free entertainment magazines found around town.

While you're at the Imperial Palace, stop by for a free souvenir photo available at the front of the casino.

Harley Davidson Café

3725 Las Vegas Boulevard South
702/740-4555
www.harley-davidsoncafe.com
Hours: Sunday through Thursday, 11 a.m. to 11 p.m.; Friday and Saturday, 11 a.m. to midnight.
Parking: There is a parking garage and valet parking at the rear of the restaurant off Harmon Avenue.

This stop will certainly be more entertaining to older male children. The café is one of those highly themed restaurants with casual food (barbecue, sandwiches, pasta) at not-so-casual prices (entrées run from $10 to $20). The restaurant, of course, is a front for a T-shirt and souvenir shop offering a world of expensive Harley merchandise. The decor is a treat for Harley lovers. An oversized Softail appears to burst through the façade on the front of the building. Seven of the latest Harley-Davidson models float around the café on a conveyer belt and lots of memorabilia from the company's century-long history adorn the walls. A seven-ton American flag made from chains hangs from the ceiling. Bar stools are replicas of motorcycle seats.

King Tut's Tomb and Museum
Luxor Las Vegas
3900 Las Vegas Boulevard South
702/262-4555
www.luxor.com
Hours: Sunday through Thursday, 9 a.m. to 11 p.m.; Friday and
Saturday, 9 a.m. to midnight.

Take a 15-minute self-guided walking tour of a replica of
the famous tomb of King Tutankhamen. The museum was developed by Egyptian sculptor and artist Dr. Mohamud Mabrook
from notes and photos taken by Howard Carter, one of the ar-
cheologists who discovered the tomb. Every detail is claimed
to have been meticulously recreated. The exhibit includes
full-scale replicas of the king's sarcophagus, guardian statues,
vases, beds, baskets, pottery, and other artifacts. The audio tour
is available in English, Spanish, French, German, and Japanese.
Admission is $5 per person.

Thrills and Chills

Las Vegas is quickly becoming the thrill ride capital of the
world. The rides provide yet another reason to visit one hotel
or another. Grownups seem to enjoy them as much as the kids
so they make great family entertainment. Here, from north to
south, are the stomach-turners available for your pleasure.

Stratosphere Tower and Thrill Rides

2000 Las Vegas Boulevard South
702/380-7777
www.stratospherehotel.com
Hours: Sunday through Thursday, 10 a.m. to 1 a.m.; Friday and
Saturday, 10 a.m. to 2 a.m.
Parking: Valet parking is recommended at the Stratosphere.
The neighborhood is a bit rough at this end of the Strip.

The Stratosphere Tower is an attraction unto itself. I'll discuss each of the rides and other attractions separately, but I'll
start with the tower, a 1,149-foot structure with an observation
deck, restaurant and bar, and rides. From indoor and outdoor
observation decks, visitors can see the entire Las Vegas Valley.
The inside deck offers coin-operated telescopes for a closer look.
The view of the Las Vegas Strip at night is spectacular, especially around dusk, but I prefer
the view of the surrounding
mountains in the daylight.

Observation Deck (above), courtesy
Nevada Commission on Tourism

Stratosphere Tower (right), courtesy
Stratosphere Hotel and Casino

Just above the observation deck is the Top of the World Restaurant. It's expensive, but the dining area revolves 360 degrees in an hour for a complete view. The elevator ride to the observation deck could be considered a thrill ride. The ride is a quick one considering the distance covered, and a little disorienting. The elevator operators are friendly and joke around with the visitors while providing background information on the tower. The elevator ride to the top of the tower is $9 for visitors and $6 for Nevada residents, seniors, and children four to 12. Children three and younger are admitted free.

Thrill Rides
(Big Shot, High Roller, X Scream, and Insanity: The Ride)
Hours: Sunday through Thursday, 10 a.m. to 1 a.m.; Friday and Saturday, 10 a.m. to 2 a.m.

The Big Shot is the famous thrill ride visited by many celebrities. The base of the ride is at the 921-foot mark on the tower. From there, riders are fired 160 feet in the air at 45 miles an hour. Powerful hydraulics stop the return drop so riders bounce a few times before the ride stops. Riders experience the force of four G's on the way up, and negative G's on the way down. The experience is quite sensational and so is the view if you dare to look, but isn't for the weak of heart. It's also not for small children. You must be 48 inches tall to ride.

Compared to the Big Shot, the High Roller roller coaster is tame. It really isn't much as far as roller coasters go; a few dips and turns, but no big deal. The thrill comes from the location. The ride dangles off the edge of the tower at 909 feet in the air. The view is great.

X Scream is shaped like a giant seesaw and passengers are strapped into the down side in an open vehicle. Then the down side goes up and riders are propelled to the other end of the seesaw 27 feet over the edge of the tower. There they dangle weightlessly above the Strip before being pulled back.

Big Shot (above), courtesy Stratosphere Hotel and Casino, High Roller Roller Coaster (below), courtesy Nevada Commission on Tourism

I'll never ride Stratosphere's newest thrill ride, Insanity: The Ride, and here's why: The hotel press material describes it as an inverted centrifuge where riders dangle 64 feet above the observation deck and spin at three G's. The ride holds 10 passengers who are loaded facing into the center of the centrifuge. As the ride begins to spin, the riders are lifted backwards so they end up facing the ground, 900 feet below, as they are slung past the edge of the observation deck.

A ride on the Big Shot, X Scream, or Insanity is $8 and the High Roller is $4. Re-rides are $4 each. Combination packages including tower admission are the best deal. They run $11.95 for tower admission and the High Roller, $15.95 for admission and either the Big Shot, X Scream, or Insanity, and $24.95 for admission and all three rides. An all-day package with unlimited rides is $29.95.

Las Vegas Cyber Speedway and Speed: The Ride

Sahara Hotel and Casino
2535 Las Vegas Boulevard South
702/734-7223

www.saharavegas.com
Hours: September through May, Monday through Thursday, noon to 9 p.m.; Friday, noon to 10 p.m.; Saturday, 11 a.m. to 10 p.m.; Sunday, 11 a.m. to 9 p.m. June through August, Sunday through Thursday, 10 a.m. to 10 p.m.; Friday and Saturday, 10 a.m. to midnight.

This is billed as the "most realistic simulated race car driving experience available." As most of us have never driven in a NASCAR race, I guess we'll just have to take their word for it. The 35,000-square-foot Cyber Speedway is located adjacent to Sahara's NASCAR Café. The cars are seven-eighths of the actual size of a stock car and mounted on hydraulic bases. A 20-foot wrap-around screen projects images from the Las Vegas Motor Speedway or a road coarse down the Las Vegas Strip. Drivers can customize the cars with 160 adjustable performance parameters such as tire pressure, wing angles, breaking response, and so forth. They can even issue instructions to the pit crew. All the thrills and chills of NASCAR racing without the danger. Children must be at least 42 inches tall. One race costs $10 and re-rides are $6.

Speed: The Ride

Hours: Sunday through Thursday, 11 a.m. to 10 p.m.; Friday and Saturday, 11 a.m. to 1 a.m.

The hotel claims this is "Las Vegas' fastest roller coaster," with speeds up to 75 mph. My assistant researchers (a group of tweens and teens) say it's pretty cool but not as cool as New York-New York's Manhattan Express. I don't usually test-ride roller coasters, but I got talked into this one. Scaring the pee-jeepers out of myself is just not my idea of entertainment. On this ride, you're shot out of the loading area toward the front of the hotel reaching a speed of 60 mph in two seconds flat (thanks to what is called "boomerang" technology). The ride takes a sharp left and zooms along the Las Vegas Strip, dives into a tunnel, then goes up into a loop. It whizzes through the Sahara marquee sign and around the porte-cochère, then straight up a 224-foot tower. At the top, the cars pause for a fraction of a second, then you take the entire ride backwards before returning to the loading area. Not my idea of fun, but the kids loved it. The cost is $10 for an unlimited number of rides. That's right, for a mere $10 you can ride till you throw up.

Note: A combo package with one ride on Speed: The Ride and one race on the Cyber Speedway is available for $15.

Speed: The Ride (left and below), courtesy Sahara Hotel and Casino

AJ Hackett Bungy

810 Circus Circus Drive
702/385-4321
www.aj-hackett.com
Hours: Vary with the season. Summer hours, Sunday through Thursday, 11 a.m. to 8:30 p.m.; Friday and Saturday, 11 a.m. to 10 p.m.
Directions: Circus Circus Drive runs north of—you guessed it—Circus Circus. AJ Hackett's is right across the street from the hotel.
Parking: Free parking is available at the facility.

Always wanted to try a bungy jump? Well, here's your chance. For more than 10 years, people have been throwing themselves off the 171-foot tower next door to Circus Circus. If you wish, and if the weather permits, the 17-story drop can end in a dip in a sparkling swimming pool. Children must be 13 years old and weigh at least 90 pounds. A parent must be present to sign a permission slip for anyone under 18. The first jump costs $54 ($59 if you want a souvenir T-shirt). After that first jump, you receive a membership card that entitles you to $25 re-jumps any time you come back. Every fourth jump is free. Hours vary so be sure to call for times.

Adventuredome

Circus Circus Hotel and Casino
2880 Las Vegas Boulevard South
702/794-3939
www.adventuredome.com
Hours: Monday through Thursday, 10 a.m. to 6 p.m.; Friday and Saturday, 10 a.m. to midnight; and Sunday, 10 a.m. to 8 p.m. Hours change with the season.
Parking: There is no convenient parking. Park in the rear of the building and walk.

Imagine, an indoor theme park. Only in Las Vegas where, of course, the high summer temperatures make air-conditioning almost mandatory. These five acres of cool comfort under a huge pink dome feature 21 rides and games for kids of all ages. You'll find a double-corkscrew roller coaster, log flume, boat ride, laser tag, IMAX film ride, climbing wall, miniature golf, and clown shows. All-day passes run from $13.95 to $19.95 depending on how tall you are (48 inches and taller pay the higher price). Individual rides run from $3 to $5. The all-day pass is the better deal, but don't count on taking all day to get what you want from the park. You can do the whole thing in two to three hours.

Canyon Blaster roller coaster (above), Rim Runner (left), and water raft ride (following page), courtesy Circus Circus Hotel and Casino

Flyaway

200 Convention Center Drive
702/731-4768
www.flyawayindoorskydiving.com
Hours: Daily, 10 a.m. to 7 p.m.
Directions: Just off the Strip, across the street from the Stardust
Hotel behind Walgreens.

This attraction simulates skydiving in a vertical wind tunnel
(the wind blows up instead of across). Flyers soar in a 12-foot-
wide column of air provided by a DC-3 propeller under netting
that serves as the floor of the well-padded 22-foot-tall tunnel.
Wind speeds go up to 130 mph, but only the most experienced
flyers go all the way to the top of the tunnel at the top speeds.
The experienced and daring can execute dips and rolls like sky-
divers.

When this attraction first opened in 1982, there were a lot of
reported accidents and it was closed for a while. New management has instituted stringent safety precautions and requires
more training for flyers. The ride is much safer than it used to be.

"We only had two broken ankles last year," a spokesperson said. That's two too many in my opinion, so be forewarned.

The session starts with a 20-minute training session, followed by a 10- to 15-minute equipment session where flyers are outfitted with a flight suit, goggles, helmet, knee and elbow pads, etc. The flight itself lasts only three minutes or so. Lots of restrictions apply. Children under 18 years of age must be accompanied by a parent. Flyers must weigh at least 40 pounds and no more than 230 pounds. Participants need to be in good physical condition with no medical, drug, or alcohol problems. Socks and soft-soled shoes are a must. No sandals or open-toed shoes are allowed.

Single flights cost $50, but the price goes down the more you fly. Two flights cost $75 and five are $150. This old granny hasn't tried it herself, but those who have say Flyaway is quite an experience.

Flyaway, courtesy Flyaway

Gondola Rides

Venetian
3377 Las Vegas Boulevard South
702/414-4525
www.venetian.com
Hours: Sunday through Thursday, 10 a.m. to 11 p.m.; Friday and Saturday, 10 a.m. to midnight.
Parking: Park in the garage on the south side of the building.

Okay, so this isn't exactly a thrill ride, but it's a great excuse to sit down and relax for a while. That might not mean much to your kids, but you'll probably need the break. Opera-singing gondoliers take you on a romantic half-mile glide in an authentic-looking Venetian gondola through the Grand Canal Shoppes on the second floor of the hotel. The ride floats beneath bridges and beside the cafés, shops, and balconies of the mall's Venetian streetscape. Rides are $12.50 for adults and $5 for children 12 and under. Children under two ride free. A private ride for two passengers is $50.

Gondola ride at the Venetian, courtesy Nevada Commission on Tourism

Cinema Ride

Forum Shops at Caesars
3500 Las Vegas Boulevard South
702/369-4008
www.cinemaride.com
Hours: Daily, 10 a.m. to midnight.

This combines motion simulation with six 3D movies. Experience "Runaway Coaster," "Atlantis Submarine Race," "Warren Miller's Ski Ride," "Haunted Graveyard Run," "Galactic Flight," or "Coaster Crazy." The five-minute rides cost $15 for one ride or $25 for all six. Must be at least 42 inches tall to ride.

Eiffel Tower Ride
> Paris Las Vegas
> 3655 Las Vegas Boulevard South
> 702/946-7000
> www.parislasvegas.com
> Hours: Daily, 10 a.m. to 1 a.m.
> Parking: Valet park at the main entrance off Las Vegas Boulevard.

Take a ride to the top of the Las Vegas version of the famous Paris landmark. The tower is rendered in meticulous detail at exactly half scale. A ride in a glass elevator to the observation deck takes you 460 feet above the ground for a nice view of the Las Vegas Strip and surrounding valley. The elevator operator serves as tour guide on the way up, pointing out special landmarks. Go at night and be sure to check out the view of the Bellagio Fountains across the street. Rides are $9 for adults and $7 for senior citizens. Children under five are free.

Eiffel Tower,
courtesy Park Place
Entertainment

Manhattan Express

New York-New York Hotel and Casino
3790 Las Vegas Boulevard South
702/740-6969
www.nynyhotelcasino.com
Hours: Sunday through Thursday, 11 a.m. to 11 p.m.; Friday and
Saturday, 10 a.m. to 11:30 p.m.; Sunday, 10 a.m. to 11:30 p.m.
Parking: Park in the garage, on the third floor if possible. A walkway connects to the level where the roller coaster is located.

My team of independent researchers (a group of tweens and
teens, plus some 40+ adults) says the Manhattan Express is the
best roller coaster in town. That evaluation excludes the death-
defying experience at Buffalo Bill's Hotel and Casino in Primm,
Nevada, about 30 miles down the highway toward Los Angeles
(see pg. 110). The Manhattan Express travels out of, over, and
around the hotel's mock-New York skyline, climbs up 203 feet,
then makes several drops including one of 144 feet at speeds
up to 67 mph. The ride features a "heartline" twist-and-dive ma-
neuver that simulates a barrel roll in a jet fighter. It rolls 180 degrees, hangs upside down 86 feet in the air, then dives back in a
loop. They take your picture during one of the drops to produce
some wonderfully flattering shots of you while screaming your
head off. The photos are available for purchase for $9.50. This
ride is not for the faint at heart or the small. Must be at least 54
inches tall to ride. Tickets are $12 each.

Manhattan Express roller coaster (facing page), courtesy MGM Mirage

Merlin's Magic Motion Machines

Excalibur Hotel and Casino
3850 Las Vegas Boulevard South
702/597-7777
www.excalibur.com
Hours: Daily, 11 a.m. to 11 p.m.

This one's scary. Elvira, Mistress of the Dark, leads you on a simulated roller coaster ride through the House of Superstition. In another ride, Craig T. Nelson leads a tour of North America's racetracks. Other rides include "The Seventh Portal," a comic adventure by Stan Lee, and "Warriors of the Dawn," a Greek mythology adventure. At $4 per ride, this is certainly the best deal among the motion simulators. Riders must be at least 42 inches tall.

In Search of the Obelisk and IMAX Theater

Luxor Las Vegas
3900 Las Vegas Boulevard South
702/262-4555
www.luxor.com
Hours: Daily, 9 a.m. to 11 p.m.

Located in the Luxor's Pharaoh's Pavilion, "In Search of the Obelisk" is a motion-simulator ride in which you visit the dig-site of a spectacular subterranean civilization. The ride starts with an all-too-realistic elevator ride where its cable snaps, plunging riders into the depths of the earth. There, riders race with the evil Dr. Osiris to save a crystal obelisk from falling into the wrong hands (though we're not sure why we care). There's a non-motion version for the queasy. The ride is a long one and so are the waiting lines. You might want to save this one for mid-week when crowds are thin. Tickets are $7.50. Children must be at least 42 inches tall to ride. Those in the know say this is one of the better motion simulators for the price.

Luxor IMAX Theater
Hours: Daily, 9 a.m. to 11 p.m.

For anyone who's been on another planet for the last few years, IMAX films are projected on a huge screen (this one is seven stories tall) using film 10 times the size of regular 35 mm. A teeth-rattling sound system along with 2D and 3D projection put viewers in the picture. Headsets have personal sound systems and 3D glasses built in. Some films shown include "Into the Deep," "Grand Canyon, The Hidden Secrets," "Space Station 3D," and "Haunted Castle." There's no admission once the film

IMAX 3D, courtesy Luxor Hotel and Casino

starts and you can't leave, either, so be sure to *go* before you go. Not recommended for children under three. Tickets are $8.95. Call to check show times.

Arcade Fun

Just about every casino/resort sports some sort of arcade. Some are more elaborate than others. Due to some incredibly unfortunate incidents where children were assaulted in arcades, security is pretty good in the hotel facilities, but it is still not recommended that you leave small children alone there. Here is a list, from north to south, of just a sampling of the more popular and elaborate arcades.

Circus Circus Midway
Circus Circus Hotel and Casino
2880 Las Vegas Boulevard South
702/734-0410
www.circuscircus.com
Hours: Daily, 11 a.m. to 11 p.m. Hours vary with the season.

Put the kids on a budget before you ever step into this place. They'll spend more than you could lose playing blackjack all night. The Midway hosts dozens of classic carnival games where you can win prizes by shooting baskets, tossing rings, and pitching baseballs. Seems to me the odds are a little better here than at your typical fair, because you see lots of people walking around with huge stuffed animals. An electronic arcade features 200 of the latest quarter-eaters.

Gameworks

Showcase Mall

3785 Las Vegas Boulevard South, Suite 010

702/432-4263

www.gameworks.com

Hours: Sunday through Thursday, 10 a.m. to midnight; Friday and Saturday, 10 a.m. to 2 a.m.

Parking: There is a parking garage to the north of the shopping center.

When Sega, Universal Studios, and Steven Spielberg's Dreamworks SKG crowd developed this concept, the idea was to have an over-the-top video arcade for adults. That's why there's a bar and a restaurant attached. That also explains why children under 18 are not admitted after 10 p.m. on weekdays and after midnight on Fridays and Saturdays. That's the time grown-ups are supposed to play. It didn't work out exactly as they had planned. The place is crammed with kids. The games are priced between 50¢ and $4. Hundreds of games range from old-time pinball to state-of-the-art blockbusters themed after the latest movies. There's also the latest in high-tech full-motion games such as Wave-Runners and Indy Cars. The Sega Power Sled is said to be the only one of its kind outside Japan and features three riders in eight-foot sleds fighting it out on a downhill snow course. One featured attraction is the 75-foot-high climbing wall called "Surge Rock." Climbs cost between $6 and $10. Gameworks operates on a "SmartCard" system where you buy your card from a dispenser and use it for games, food, or shopping, then reload it when you run out of credits. Go early; the crowd seems to get rougher and tougher later at night.

Coney Island Emporium

New York-New York Hotel and Casino
3790 Las Vegas Boulevard South
702/740-6969
www.nynyhotelcasino.com
Hours: Daily, 10 a.m. to midnight.
Parking: Park in the parking garage in back of the hotel.

This 32,000-square-foot complex features carnival games, laser tag, an eight-player Daytona-style interactive driving simulator, bumper cars, shooting galleries, and more than 200 quarter-token-operated games all done in a Coney Island motif. This arcade battles it out every year with Circus Circus for the title of "Best Arcade on the Strip" in the local paper's readers' poll and usually wins. One advantage might be location. The arcade is on a second level completely removed from the casino. It's just steps off the parking garage, so you don't even have to travel through the casino to get there. It's noisy, but the kids don't seem to mind.

Fantasy Faire Midway

Excalibur Hotel and Casino
3850 Las Vegas Boulevard South
702/597-7777
www.excalibur.com
Hours: Monday through Thursday, 11 a.m. to 11 p.m.; Friday through Sunday, 10 a.m. to midnight. Hours vary with the season.

Excalibur is a sister hotel to Circus Circus. Both are owned by Mandalay Resort Group and both sport a similar midway with carnival games and an arcade. Excalibur's is done in a medieval English motif and sports wandering performers.

3 Around the Valley

We've covered "Vegas," now we turn to Las Vegas, the metropolitan area of 1.5 million (going on 2 million) residents that includes several towns, cities, neighborhoods, and lots of unincorporated areas within Clark County. The attractions and activities found here are as diverse as the fast-growing populations—from high-brow museums to run-down petting zoos.

Again the entries have been arranged by type and, as closely as possible, grouped together geographically.

Close Encounters of a Cultural Kind

Many people who live here complain that Las Vegas has no culture. I am never quite sure what in the world they are talking about. Las Vegas has lots of culture; it may be on the weird and tacky side, but the city has a very distinct culture of its own. Following are some of the cultural experiences many locals enjoy.

Downtown and Points North

Las Vegas Natural History Museum
900 Las Vegas Boulevard North
702/384-3466
www.lvnhm.org
Hours: Daily, 9 a.m. to 4 p.m.
Directions: Drive north on Las Vegas Boulevard past Fremont Street and US 95. The museum is on the right, but look sharp; the sign is hard to see.
Parking: Lots of parking in front of the building.

My granddaughter calls this "The Dinosaur Newseum." For the little ones, the big attraction is certainly the life-size roaring robotic dinosaurs. One of my granddaughters likes to push the button to make the animals move and roar, while the other one hides behind my legs. They also get a big kick out of the pool of live sharks in the Marine Room. You can look over the edge of the tank and almost touch the sharks if you're foolish enough. Another favorite spot is the hands-on Exploration Room where the kids can dig for fossils in the sand, make tracings, and even do some pretend tracking. There's an exhibit of indigenous Nevada flora and fauna, an International Wildlife Room with a preserved grizzly bear, tiger, zebra, and stuffed giraffe. The Africa Room recreates animals from the savanna and the rainforest. This is not the world's greatest museum, but it tries hard. You won't have to worry about crowds or about your kids disturbing other visitors. There are rarely many people there. Older kids might find this kind of lame, but the little ones will love it. The Old Mormon Fort is right next door, so you might as well check out both at once. Admission is $6 for adults; $5 for seniors, students 11 and over, and military; and $3 for children three to 11. Children two years and under are free.

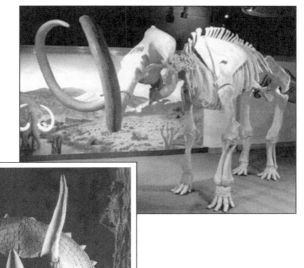

Fossils (above), Triceratops (left) and Leopard sharks (below), courtesy Las Vegas Natural History Museum

Old Las Vegas Mormon Fort State Historical Park

500 East Washington Avenue
702/486-3511
www.parks.nv.gov/olvmf.htm
Hours: Daily, 8 a.m. to 4:30 p.m.
Directions: Drive north on Las Vegas Boulevard past Fremont Street and US 95. The fort is on the right on the southeast corner of Las Vegas Boulevard North and Washington Avenue.

Just a few years after the Mormons settled Salt Lake City, church president Brigham Young sent settlers to lay claim to the trickle of water known as Las Vegas Creek and to convert the local Indians. In 1855, a group of 29 settlers built an adobe fort for protection. The mission lasted only a couple of years before it and the lead-mining operation that followed shortly were abandoned. The fort passed through the hands of several subsequent settlers until the walls and foundation of one of the buildings were used to build a ranch house that today is the oldest building in Nevada.

The ranch house serves as the visitors' center at the park. It contains photos and text panels detailing the fort's history and authentic furniture, including a pump organ, spinning wheel, and butter churn. The display also includes the first flag flown over Las Vegas, made from denim and an old red shirt. Other parts of the old fort have been recreated. This is a great place to get a glimpse of what settling the West was really like. It was nowhere near as glamorous as the cowboy legends, but quite an accomplishment just the same. I enjoy history, so I love this place, but children may get bored quickly. You can combine the trip with a visit to the Lied Museum across the street as a compromise. The admission fee is only $2 for adults and $1 for children six to 12 (under six free), so you won't mind if the kids don't want to stay long.

Lied Discovery Children's Museum

833 Las Vegas Boulevard North
702/382-5437
www.ldcm.org
Hours: Tuesday through Sunday, 10 a.m. to 5 p.m.
Directions: From the Strip, drive north on Las Vegas Boulevard past downtown. The museum is just past US 95 on the left.

This is a hands-on science, art, and natural history museum much like you find in most big cities. Here businesses, artists, and public entities have sponsored some of the exhibits. A local grocery chain has sponsored a mock store, for instance, and the performing arts group Blue Man Group has sponsored an unusual tunnel playhouse. Children can stack boxes to create a house or fort, feel their weight on a different planet, or dress up in costumes and perform on a stage with curtains. I was surprised at how much the four-year-olds enjoyed playing bank and grocery store. A favorite of all the kids was a photosensitive wall that captures shadows in a flash of light. "Desert Discovery," a special area for little kids, lets children work as miners at the fic-

Science Day, courtesy Lied Discovery Museum

tional Boulder Mountain where they mine the pits, deposit ore in the buckets, and send it down the mountain on a hand-cranked conveyer. Just about everything is hands-on except for a display of two huge elaborate dollhouses enclosed in cases.

The place seems shopworn and ragged around the edges. Many of the exhibits didn't work during a recent visit. The ATM at the bank was out of order, as was a world map that was supposed to play snippets of the languages spoken at various exotic locations. But the admission price is reasonable and the experience overall is still worth the cost. Admission is $6 for adults; $5 for seniors 55 and older, children under 18, and military. Children under one are free. Children under 11 must be accompanied by an adult.

Walker African-American Museum

705 West Van Buren Street
702/649-2238
Hours: Tours by appointment only.
Directions: Take Las Vegas Boulevard north past Fremont Street and US 95 to Bonanza Road; turn left. Take Bonanza to H Street and turn right. About six blocks north on H Street, the museum is on the southeast corner of H Street and West Van Buren Street.

The contribution of African-Americans to carving a metropolis from the desert wilderness has been sadly neglected, but this museum hopes to change all that. The Walker museum houses a 10,000-piece collection of artifacts from the lives of famous and not-so-famous African-Americans. The current collection is a hodgepodge of items from all over the country, but soon the museum will concentrate on the lives of African-Americans who helped settle Nevada. The collection is currently housed in a converted home in the heart of the city's older

Westside neighborhood. An active committee of volunteers is working to raise money for a permanent facility. Admission is $1 for everyone.

Center City

Nevada State Museum and Historical Society

700 Twin Lakes Drive
702/486-5205
www.nevadaculture.org
Hours: Daily, 9 a.m. to 5 p.m., except Thanksgiving, Christmas, and New Year's Day.
Directions: Take Las Vegas Boulevard north past Fremont Street and US 95. Turn left on Washington Avenue. Take Washington Avenue to Twin Lakes Drive on the left (past Rancho Drive). The sign for Twin Lakes Drive is hard to see, so be on the lookout. The museum is located in Lorenzi Park.

This is one of those places most visitors never see. It's a little out of the way but not really very far from the tourist corridor. This nationally accredited museum displays artifacts, graphics, and photos covering the history of Las Vegas from prehistoric times to present day. Exhibits cover the history of gambling, the building of Hoover Dam, and the good old days of above-ground atomic testing. Displays cover anthropology, history, and natural history. If you make the effort to find this place, be sure to take a little time. There's lots to see here, including mining displays, a wooly mammoth skeleton, and the Benjamin "Don't call me Bugsy" Siegel suite from the old Flamingo Hotel. Admission is free for children under 18 and general admission is $2.

Desert Demonstration Garden

3701 West Alta Drive
702/258-3205
www.lvspgardens.org
Hours: Daily, 8 a.m. to 5 p.m.
Directions: From Las Vegas Boulevard, take Sahara Avenue west to Valley View Boulevard; turn right. Take Valley View Boulevard past Charleston Boulevard. The Demonstration Garden is on the right at the corner of Valley View and Alta Drive.

Desert Demonstration Garden, courtesy Southern Nevada Water Authority

This is another out-of-the-way oasis that even few locals ever visit. The Desert Demonstration Garden is located near what's left of the springs that created the meadows for which Las Vegas was named. The area, which runs along the south side of US 95 from about Rancho Drive to Valley View Boulevard, was the site of some of the first settlements in the valley. The springs are now owned and protected by the Southern Nevada Water Authority. The 3.5-acre garden was created by the Water Authority to teach homeowners how to landscape using water-efficient plants. A series of paths winds through 12 separate gardens with more than 1,000 species of plants. The Native

Wash features plants native to the area. You'll look at the desert differently after you visit this little oasis. Gardeners are on hand Thursdays and Saturdays from 9 a.m. to 1 p.m. to answer questions. There are a series of gardening classes offered, but they are geared to adults. The gardens make a nice relaxing getaway for families.

Henderson

Clark County Heritage Museum
1830 Boulder Highway
702/455-7955
www.co.clark.nv.us/parks/Clark_County_Museum.htm
Hours: Daily, 9 a.m. to 4:30 p.m.
Directions: Take I-15 south to I-215. Take I-215 east until it turns into Lake Mead Drive and crosses US 95. Turn right on Boulder Highway. The museum is on the left, past Race Track Road. (Don't be fooled, there is no racetrack, just a road.)

At only $1 for kids and $1.50 for adults, this might be one of the best entertainment bargains in the valley. The indoor part of the museum is nicely executed with displays and dioramas de-

Clark County Heritage Museum, courtesy Clark County Parks and Community Services Division

picting the history of the valley from prehistoric Native-American civilizations through the pioneer days to the more current "Age of Entertainment," including, of course, an exhibit on gambling. Traveling exhibits are displayed in one large room. A recent example was a collection of hand fans from the last century and before. The most fun is Heritage Street, a collection of seven historic homes and buildings that have been moved to the museum site and restored. There's a 1900s newspaper print shop, an old railroad cottage, and homes from the '30s and '50s (remember, Las Vegas doesn't have much history from before 1930). Across the lane from Heritage Street is a restored barn, a railroad depot, and a ghost town of old mining cottages and outbuildings all connected by a walking trail. There are wagons, old vehicles, and way more than there is space to list here. It's a great history lesson and fun to boot. The museum is operated by the Clark County Parks and Community Services Division.

Ethel M® Chocolate Factory & Botanical Cactus Garden

2 Cactus Garden Drive
702/458-8864
www.ethelm.com
Hours: Daily, 8:30 a.m. to 7 p.m., except Christmas and Thanksgiving.
Directions: Take Las Vegas Boulevard south to Sunset Road; turn left. Take Sunset Road through Green Valley until the road ends in a T. The factory is just ahead to the left.

The "M" in Ethel M® stands for Mars, the makers of Snickers and M&M's. And in this case, the "M" also stands for "mmmm." Through large glass windows, watch workers create the fine chocolates all chocolate lovers know and love. In one room, you see workers create some of the 50 different centers used in the candies, one batch at a time. In others, you'll actually see the yummy centers being covered with rich, creamy chocolate or

Ethel M® production line, courtesy M&M Mars Company

the making of hard chocolate shells to be filled with soft liqueur centers. Lastly, you'll view the packaging room, where the candies are individually wrapped in foil, and then you'll finally get the free sample you've been longing for. Outside the factory is a three-acre cactus garden with more than 350 species of cactus, desert plants, and trees. The garden is also the site of a waste-water recycling center that cleans water from the factory to use on the garden.

Ron Lee's World of Clowns

7665 Commercial Way, Suite A
702/434-1700
www.ronlee.com
Hours: Monday through Friday, 9 a.m. to 4 p.m.; closed Saturday, Sunday, and holidays.
Directions: Take Las Vegas Boulevard south to Warm Springs Road; turn left. The World of Clowns is on the corner of Warm Springs Road and Gibson Road.

The World of Clowns is a factory where artists produce clown figurines and statues for Warner Brothers, Disney, and other companies to resell in their own retail shops. Visitors take a self-guided tour of the pink circus-tent-shaped factory to see the workers making molds and putting detail touches on the pieces. A video, if it's running properly, explains the creative process that goes into making each piece. After the tour, take in the collection of circus memorabilia, including clothing worn by famous circus clowns, clown props, circus posters, and more. The tour is free, but the location is a bit remote (about 10 miles from the Strip). This may not be worth a special trip unless you really love clowns, but you might want to stop by if you are in the Henderson area.

North Las Vegas

CCSN Planetarium
3200 East Cheyenne Avenue
702/651-4759
www.ccsn.nevada.edu
Hours: Shows are Friday, 6 and 7:30 p.m. and Saturday, 3:30 and 7:30 p.m.
Directions: Take I-15 north to Cheyenne Avenue, turn right. The Community College of Southern Nevada campus is on the left. The planetarium is located just inside the south entrance.

Each session at the planetarium is a double feature, including a rotating program plus "Star Watch," a look at the sky as it appears that evening. The regular program runs a little more than 30 minutes and "Star Watch" runs 20 minutes or so. After each 7:30 p.m. show, telescopes in the student observatory are available for the "Sky Watch Live" program for up-close looks at the moon, stars, and planets. Planetarium brochures caution that the observatory is open "weather permitting," but it's a rare day in Las Vegas that the sky is not clear. Be sure to call or visit the Web site for current show listings. Admission is $5 for adults and $3 for seniors over 55, children under 12, and CCSN students.

Carroll Shelby Museum

6755 Speedway Boulevard
702/942-7325
www.shelbyautos.com
Hours: Monday through Friday, 8 a.m. to 4 p.m. Free tours at 10:30 a.m.
Directions: Located at the entrance to the Las Vegas Motor Speedway. Take I-15 north to Speedway Boulevard, exit 54.

Remember the Shelby Cobra from the 1960s? No, you probably don't, because parents of today's children weren't even born at the time. Granny here was a mere child herself. If cars, fast ones, are your thing, you can't pass this place up. The museum, part of the Shelby Company's 100,000-square-foot manufacturing facility, displays 40 years of Shelby performance cars including the 1962 model that started it all and the new Series 1. The tour includes a peek into the plant where the cars are being built. Boys of driving age, or those who wish they were, will love

1961 Shelby Cobra, courtesy Shelby Company

this. It's a nice excuse for race fans to check out the speedway, home of the UAW-Daimler Chrysler 400 held each March.

Thunderbird Museum

Nellis Air Force Base
Tyndall Avenue
702/652-7200
www.airforce.com/thunderbirds
Hours: Tours by appointment Monday through Friday only, 8 a.m. to 4 p.m. Closed on holidays.
Directions: Take I-15 north to Craig Road, then turn right. Craig Road runs directly into the main gate at the base. Stop at the visitor's center for further information.

Thunderbirds, courtesy United States Air Force

Even before 9/11 you practically needed CIA security clearance to get to see this museum dedicated to the Air Force poster boys, the Thunderbirds. Right now, even that wouldn't do it; the museum is open only to retired or active military personnel who already have access to the base. The display is a collection of personal items and photos of the pilots and the various celebrities who have been allowed to fly with them. The tour includes (or used to) a peek into the Thunderbird hangar for a close-up look at one of the team's $23 million red, white, and blue F-16Cs. There's a short video on the team. Right now, the museum is open to groups of 20 or more only and is not recommended for children under 12. There is no transportation provided from the Main Gate to the Thunderbird Hangar, but they will give you directions. I'm not sure it's worth all this, but if you go, be sure to ask directions to the I Street gate to see the airplanes on display at POW/MIA Freedom Park.

Airport Area

Liberace Museum
1775 East Tropicana Avenue
702/798-5595
www.liberace.com
Hours: Monday through Saturday, 10 a.m. to 5 p.m.; Sunday, noon to 4 p.m. Closed Thanksgiving, Christmas, and New Year's Day.
Directions: From Las Vegas Boulevard, take Tropicana Avenue (conveniently next to the Tropicana Hotel) east past Maryland Parkway. The museum is on the right.

Although Liberace died before today's children were born, his museum is included in the listings because he was a mainstay of Las Vegas entertainment for so many years. Besides, they say he was an incredibly nice man. (I never met him myself, but I know people who did.) The non-profit museum was founded by Mr. Showmanship himself in 1979 to raise funds for the Liberace Foundation for the Performing and Creative Arts. The collection includes Liberace's jewelry and costumes, for which the word "flamboyant" was invented. Of course, there's the famous candelabra that was his trademark and his rhinestone-covered grand piano. In fact, 18 of Liberace's 39 pianos are on display. Then there's the car collection, including the Rolls Royce covered with mirror tiles and etched with a galloping horse. I've never taken a child to this museum, but maybe I should. How do you keep a legend alive if you don't tell the kids about it? Admission is $12 for adults, $8 for seniors 65 and older and children six and up (including college students with ID). Children five and under are free. Tip: If you arrive by bus or taxi, show a receipt to get $2 off the admission fee, though that doesn't make this worth the cost of a cab ride.

Liberace's extravagent wardrobe (right) and piano room (below), courtesy Liberace Museum

UNLV Barrick Museum of Natural History

4505 Maryland Parkway
702/895-3381
http://hrcweb.nevada.edu/Museum/hrc
Hours: Monday through Friday, 8 a.m. to 4:45 p.m. and Saturday, 10 a.m. to 2 p.m.
Directions and Parking: From the Las Vegas Strip, take Harmon Avenue (between the Aladdin and the Harley-Davidson Café) east. Keep going past the Hard Rock Hotel until the road dead-ends in a parking lot on the UNLV campus. The museum is to the right, on the south side of the parking lot.

This is a quiet out-of-the-way spot. The museum's exhibits focus on Southwestern and Central American native cultures and the exotic landscape of the Mojave Desert. Glass terrariums display live snakes, lizards, and desert tortoises. Exhibits show examples of artifacts and art by Native American cultures such as the Southern Paiute, Navajo, and Hopi. Other rotating exhibits include displays on Las Vegas, the building of Hoover Dam,

Marjorie Barrick Museum of Natural History, courtesy UNLV

pre-Columbian cultures, and dance masks of Mexico and of the Huipils of Guatemala. The main exhibit hall also features a 2,500-square-foot temporary and traveling exhibit area, which hosts international, national, and regional exhibits that change every eight weeks. Older children will enjoy this. Admission is free.

UNLV Arboretum

4505 Maryland Parkway
702/895-3392
http://www.unlv.edu/facilities/landscape/arboretum.html
Directions and Parking: The UNLV Campus lies between Flamingo Road, Tropicana Avenue, Paradise Road, and Maryland Parkway. Easiest access from the Strip is to take Tropicana Avenue east past Swenson Street and park in the Thomas and Mack Arena parking lot.

This is a great place to go to let the kids run, ride their skateboards and bikes, and just let loose. It's best to go on the weekend or on a holiday when school is not in session, parking is available, and things are a little quieter. Between early December and late January, for example, the campus is completely shut down except for administrative staff. Evenings and weekends are also a good time to visit.

The entire 335-acre campus is an official state arboretum. Hundreds of trees shade acres of emerald-green grass. It's a refreshing change from the desert and the concrete canyons of the tourist corridor.

While you're there, be sure to stop by the Xeric Garden just outside the Barrick Museum (above). The place gives new meaning to the idea of desert landscaping. The garden contains plants from the arid regions of Australia, South America, Mexico, and the Mediterranean with a nice helping from the North American deserts. The plants are labeled with little signs for identification. Many of the plants bloom all year, but in the spring it's an especially glorious place. There are benches and paths and bird-viewing ramada with a fountain and pool.

Guided tours of the campus grounds are available upon request.

Howard W. Cannon Aviation Museum

McCarran Airport
702/455-7968
www.co.clark.nv.us/parks/Clark_County_Museum.htm
Directions: From the Strip, take Tropicana Avenue east to Paradise Road. Turn right and follow the signs.

Visitors won't have to go much out of their way to see this exhibit and locals can check it out while waiting for company to arrive (we locals get lots of visitors). It's located on the airport's

Howard W. Cannon
Aviation Museum,
courtesy Cannon Aviation Museum

second level, above baggage claim. Other displays are located throughout the airport. The museum is named for a long-time United States senator who championed the development of aviation services in the valley. The museum shows the history of aviation in Clark County from the first flight in 1920 through the introduction of the jet. There are lots of old photos, pilot uniforms, aviation artwork, and even an old mail plane. The collection isn't extensive, but it's interesting and it's free.

Here's a little side trip. Take Las Vegas Boulevard south past Mandalay Bay to Sunset Road and turn left. On the left hand side of the road, you'll see a turnout where you can park and watch the planes land. Tune your radio to 88.5 FM and you can listen to the pilots talk to the tower as they come in. Great outing for a summer evening.

Up Close and Personal with Animals

It's a rare child who doesn't love animals, at least in the abstract. Although Las Vegas isn't known for having elaborate facilities for wildlife (at least outside the tourist areas), the petting zoos and wildlife viewing areas that do exist provide a more intimate experience than the attractions on the Strip.

Southern Nevada Zoological-Botanical Park
1775 North Rancho Drive
702/647-4685
www.lasvegaszoo.org
Hours: Daily, 9 a.m. to 5 p.m.
Directions: Take US 95 north to Rancho Drive; turn right. The zoo is on the left just past Vegas Drive.

The San Diego Zoo it isn't, but there is a nice collection of endangered cats, including a lion and a tiger, other exotic and native animals, and what they claim is the last family of Barbary apes in the United States. You can see eagles, ostriches, emus, talking parrots, wallabies, flamingos, and large exotic reptiles. An alligator lives in a pool with a glass panel in the side so you get a good up-close look. A reptile house displays every species of venomous reptile native to Southern Nevada. The zoo also features exhibits by the Las Vegas Gem Club and botanical displays of endangered cycads and rare bamboos. The zoo is clean and the animals appear to be well cared for. Like similar activities on the Strip, you're forced to go through the gift shop to reach the exit; a cheap trick, to my way of thinking. General admission is $6.50; children two to 12 and seniors 62 and older are $4.50. Children under two are free.

Tip: There is a printable coupon for half-price admission for a child with a paying adult on the Web site.

Southern Nevada Zoological-Botanical Park, photo by Pat Dingle, courtesy Southern Nevada Zoo

Gilcrease Nature Sanctuary
8103 Racel Street
702/645-4224
Hours: Wednesday through Sunday, 10 a.m. to 3 p.m.
Directions: Take US 95 north past Ann Road to Durango; turn right. Take Durango to Racel; turn right.

The nature sanctuary houses displaced birds and animals that have been abandoned by their owners. The collection includes domestic and indigenous wildlife such as quail, pheasants, turkeys, peacocks, and lots of colorful and unusual-looking chickens housed in large cages. A small petting zoo is home to goats and an emu. A small pond plays host to hundreds of wa-

Gilcrease Nature Sanctuary, photos by Jim Foster, courtesy Montgomery Watson Harza

terfowl, including swans removed from local golf courses. The sanctuary is located on land once farmed by the Gilcrease family, who came to the area in 1920. The reserve was started more than 25 years ago by Bill Gilcrease, now in his 80s. The park is rustic and smells funny. Advertised rates are $3 for adults and $1 for children, but sometimes they jack up the admission for out-of-towners. You can look at your admission as a contribution to the sanctuary's good works. They even rescue pigeons removed from the tourist corridor for making a mess of the fancy buildings.

Gilcrease Nature Sanctuary, photo by Jim Foster, courtesy Montgomery Watson Harza

Henderson Bird Viewing Preserve

2400-B Moser Drive
Henderson
www.cityofhenderson.com/parks/facilities/BVP/php/Bird
Preserve.php
Hours: Daily, 6 a.m. to 3 p.m.
Directions: From the Las Vegas Strip, take Tropicana Avenue east to Eastern Avenue and turn right. Take Eastern Avenue to Sunset Road and turn left. Take Sunset Road past US 93 and turn left on Moser Drive. Follow Moser Drive as it makes a sharp turn and go to the second gate. Dial #100 in the security gate keypad and someone will let you in.

If there were Academy Awards for animal preserves, this one might get the prize for "Best Use of a Sewage Treatment

Facility." It's not as yucky as it sounds. The Bird Viewing Preserve is located on the evaporative ponds that hold treated water before it flows back into Lake Mead. The preserve has, in fact, won awards from the US Environmental Protection Agency for providing a haven for more than 200 native and migratory birds. Viewing is best in the cooler months, October through April, but there's something to see all year round. An early-morning visit in the summer is pleasant, but plan to be back in the air conditioning by 9 a.m. During the winter, this is a good place to see herons, shorebirds, and gulls. You might even spot migrating flycatchers, swallows, and sparrows. This site also attracts desert species such as Gambel's quail, sage sparrow, crissal thrasher, and black-chinned hummingbird. If you're lucky, you might see hawks or falcons. Because the preserve is part of the valley's water treatment system, it's closed any time the national terror alert status goes to orange or red. Admission is free.

Clark County Wetlands Park

7050 Wetlands Park Lane
Henderson
702/455-7522
www.co.clark.nv.us/parks/Wetlands/Wetland%27s_Home page.htm
Hours: The preserve is open dawn to dusk. The Visitors' Center is open from 10 a.m. to 4 p.m. daily.
Directions: From Las Vegas Boulevard, take Tropicana Avenue east, 1.5 miles past Boulder Highway.

The wetlands sit on the Las Vegas Wash, a channel that takes runoff water from the city to Lake Mead. The wetlands cover 2,900 acres and the county has developed about 130 acres into a nature preserve and wetlands park. Facilities include an information center and five miles of walking trails of various lengths. A two-mile hike takes you along a stream and around ponds ringed with riparian and wetland plants. For the more hearty, a three-mile gravel trail leads to a series of ponds that provide habitat for many migratory birds. Volunteers are available at the Visitors' Center to answer questions or provide guided tours. This is a great place for walking, jogging, hiking, and observing wildlife.

Clark County Wetlands Park, courtesy Clark County Parks and Community Services Division

Faster, Higher

The Las Vegas Strip doesn't have a monopoly on thrill rides. Around the valley you will find several attractions where the "need for speed" can be satisfied. Most of these activities will be for older children, but some can accommodate little ones too.

Las Vegas Mini Gran Prix

1401 North Rainbow Boulevard
702/259-7000
www.lvmgp.com
Hours: Daily, 10 a.m. to 10 p.m.
Directions: Take US 95 north to Lake Mead East. Turn right on Rainbow Boulevard and continue to Vegas Drive.

There's something here for kids of all ages, but the older kids will especially enjoy it. Four driving tracks include a kiddie-cart oval for the very young (four and under), go-carts, an oval "sprint" course, and a mini-gran-prix curving course. The gran-prix course is reserved for licensed drivers 16 and older. Other attractions include a burlap sack slide, a dragon-themed roller coaster, and a tornado ride similar to Disney's teacups. There's also an arcade and snack bar. Some might consider this place expensive. Tickets are $4.95 and the driving rides (except the kiddie carts) are one ticket each. The roller coaster, slide, kiddie carts, and tornado are half a ticket. A packet of five tickets goes for the slightly discounted price of $22.50.

Derek Daly Performance Driving Academy
7055 Speedway Boulevard, Suite E102
Las Vegas Motor Speedway
702/643-2126
www.derekdaly.com
Hours: Daily, 7 a.m. to 5 p.m.
Directions: Take I-15 north to Speedway Boulevard, Exit 54.

This is definitely one for the older kids, but special thrills are available for children who weigh more than 50 pounds. Any licensed driver 16 or older who can handle a basic manual transmission can take a class in performance race driving. The training starts with about an hour's worth of classroom lessons and practice in the "accident-avoidance simulator." The training is followed by a car-control clinic in the BMW skid car. Next you take the wheel of a Formula Ford 2000 or a BMW Z3 Roadster to try your newly acquired skills. Tuition starts at $600 for a half-day session and climbs to $4,200 for a four-day program. Anyone big enough to ride in a car without a car seat can participate as a ride-along in a race starting at $100 each, but these require a group of five or more. Call for reservations.

XPlex Las Vegas Kart Racing
15000 Las Vegas Boulevard South
Sloan
702/260-6355
www.lasvegaskarting.com
Hours: Vary. Summer hours are Tuesday through Sunday, 3 p.m. to 11 p.m.
Directions: Take I-15 south 12 miles to the Sloan exit (Exit 25). Make a left off the exit, then a right on Las Vegas Boulevard. The track is on the left.

These go-karts have nothing to do with the four-wheeled

gizmos powered by lawn-mower motors that my dad built in the middle of the last century. The top-of-the-line 125cc 6-speed Shifter Kart can go up to 100 miles an hour. You can rent a tamer Kid Kart for children ages five to seven or the Junior Kart for eight- to 11-year-olds for $75 per half hour. There's also a 6.5-hp Spitfire Kart that goes for $30 for 15 minutes or $50 per half-hour. Prices go up to $225 per half-hour for the shifter. For the faster models, you must be 16 years old and have a driver's license. Driving lessons start at $150 for little kids and go up to $855 for a full day on the Shifter Kart. Reservations are required.

Be a Sport

Active fun may be the best of all. Build strong healthy bodies, improve coordination, run off that excess energy, improve self confidence, and have a great time doing it. Following are some participatory activities you and you children can enjoy together.

Bowling

Bowling is a staple attraction in many of the casinos that focus on local business. Since it's pretty much the same wherever you go, I won't review all the bowling alleys in town. Instead, I'll list them all, focusing on the three named the best in the *Las Vegas Review-Journal* reader's poll. They all have pro shops, snack bars, electronic scoring, and all the other features you would find in a modern bowling alley. At press time, Sunset Station opened a state-of-the-art bowling facility.

Texas Station Bowling Center

2101 Texas Star Lane
702/631-8128
www.texasstation.com
Hours: 24 hours, seven days a week. Cosmic bowling takes place on Fridays, 9 p.m. to 2 a.m.; Saturdays, 5 p.m. to 2 a.m.; and Sundays, noon to 5 p.m.

This is a practically brand new facility with 60 lanes and state-of-the-art equipment. Readers of the local paper rated this one the best. Special "Cosmic Bowling" sessions every weekend include a light and sound show to jazz up the lanes. Recreational bowlers are welcome almost anytime except during large tournaments. Games are $2 for adults and $1 for children under 12 from midnight to 5 p.m. daily and $2.75 and $1.75 in the evenings, except for Cosmic Bowling nights. Cosmic Bowling is $3.75 for adults and $2.75 for children on Friday and Saturday and $2.75 for everyone on Sunday. Shoes are $2. Call ahead to make sure lanes are available.

Orleans Bowling Center

4500 West Tropicana Avenue
702/365-7400
www.orleanscasino.com
Hours: 24 hours, seven days a week.
Directions: From the Las Vegas Strip, take Tropicana Avenue west. The Orleans is located at the corner of Tropicana and Arville Street.

The Orleans Bowling Center was named the best in Las Vegas for years until the Texas Station claimed the title last year. It has 70 state-of-the-art lanes and $1 games and drinks from midnight to 8 a.m. Sunday through Thursday. Regular rates are $2.75 for adults and $1.75 for children under 16 and seniors 55 and over, except on Saturdays, Sundays, and holidays when everyone pays $2.75. Shoe rentals are $2.25.

Suncoast Bowling Center
9090 Alta Drive
702/636-7400
www.suncoastcasino.com
Hours: 24 hours, seven days a week.
Directions: Take US 95 north to Summerlin Parkway. Exit Summerlin Parkway at Rampart Road; turn left. The Suncoast is on the right.

Suncoast is owned by the same company that owns and operates the Orleans, so the prices and specials are the same as above. This facility offers "Cosmic Bowling" with a light show and music on Friday and Saturday nights, but it's more expensive than Texas Station's at $4 per game and $2 for shoes. The editors of the *Las Vegas Review-Journal* named the Suncoast Bowling Center "Best of Las Vegas."

Other Local Bowling Facilities

Gold Coast Bowling Center
4000 West Flamingo Road
702/367-4700
www.goldcoastcasinos.com

Mahoney's Silver Nugget Bowling Center
2140 Las Vegas Boulevard North
North Las Vegas
702/320-2695
www.mahoneyscasino.com

Bowling Center, courtesy Sam's Town Gambling Hall and Casino

Sam's Town Bowling Center

5111 Boulder Highway
702/456-7777
www.samstownlv.com

Santa Fe Station Bowling Center

4949 North Rancho Drive
702/658-4900
www.stationcasinos.com

Sunset Lanes and Casino

4451 East Sunset Road
Henderson
702/736-2695
www.renatas.com

Sunset Station

1301 West Sunset Road
Henderson
702/547-7777
www.sunsetstation.com

Terrible's Town Casino & Bowl
642 South Boulder Highway
Henderson
702/564-7118

Skating

Athletic Arts Academy
6150 Annie Oakley Drive
702/450-2787
www.athleticartsacademy.com
Hours: Wednesday and Friday, 6 to 8 p.m.; Saturday, 1 to 3 p.m.
and 3 to 5 p.m.; and Sunday, noon to 2 p.m. and 2 to 4 p.m.
Directions: Take Las Vegas Boulevard south to Sunset Road;
turn left. Take Sunset Road to Annie Oakley Drive.

This is a studio built by Peter Foy, the theatrical flying expert
who has hoisted everyone from the Flying Nun to the Backstreet
Boys. This venture is dedicated to teaching all kinds of theatrical
athleticism, including ice skating. The academy opens its por-
table ice rink to the public several times per week. Skating is $6
per two-hour session and skate rentals are $2.

Fiesta Rancho Ice Arena
4949 North Rancho Drive
702/647-7465
www.fiestacasino.com
Hours: Vary according to leagues and private events booked;
generally Tuesday through Friday, 3:30 to 5:30 p.m. and Saturday and Sunday, 1 to 3 p.m.
Directions: Take US 95 north to the Lake Mead Boulevard exit.
The hotel is located on the northeast corner of Lake Mead and
Rancho Drive.

This arena-sized ice rink hosts hockey leagues and skating lessons and is open to the public when other events are not booked. Be sure to call ahead because open skating times vary month to month. Admission is $6. Skate rental is $2.50. On Sundays, skating and rentals are $5.

Crystal Palace Roller Skating

3901 North Rancho Drive
702/645-4892
www.skatevegas.com
Hours: Vary. Summer, Tuesday through Thursday, 11 a.m. to 4 p.m. and 7 to 9:30 p.m.; Friday, 7 to 11 p.m.; Saturday, 2 to 11 p.m.; and Sunday, 2 to 5 p.m.
Directions: Take US 95 north to Craig Road. At the exit, turn right. Take Craig Road east to Rancho Drive; turn left. The rink is on the left.

The rink features wood floors, light systems, and DJs. Weekday admission is $7 with a $1 discount if you have your own skates. Weekend rates are $8 with a $1 discount with your own skates.

Crystal Palace Roller Skating

4680 Boulder Highway
702/458-7107
www.skatevegas.com
Hours: Vary. Summer hours, Tuesday through Thursday, 1 to 4 p.m. and 7 to 10 p.m.; Friday, 7 to 11 p.m.; Saturday, 2 to 11 p.m.; and Sunday, 2 to 5 p.m. and 7 to 10 p.m.
Directions: Take Flamingo Road east to Boulder Highway. Turn left. The rink is one mile on the left.

This one's older than the Rancho Drive location but closer

to the Strip. Weekday admission is $7 with a $1 discount if you have your own skates. Weekend rates are $8 with a $1 discount with your own skates. Wednesday is Family Night and a family of four can skate for $12 if a parent buys the tickets.

Other Fun Stuff

Funworks Family Fun Center
2050 Olympic Avenue
Henderson
702/454-4386
Hours: Vary with the season. Summer hours, Monday through Thursday, 10 a.m. to 10 p.m.; Friday and Saturday, 11 a.m. to 11 p.m.; and Sunday, noon to 10 p.m.
Directions: Take Las Vegas Boulevard south to Sunset Road; turn left. Take Sunset Road past Green Valley Parkway. Funworks is behind Barley's Casino on the left.

Kids will have hours of fun with a variety of activities, including an indoor roller-skating rink, go-carts, bumper boats, and two 18-hole putt-putt courses. The facility also houses a large video arcade and a snack bar.

Laser Quest
7361 West Lake Mead Boulevard
702/243-8881
www.laserquest.com
Hours: Hours vary with the season. Summer hours, Tuesday through Thursday, 6 to 9 p.m.; Friday, 4 to 11 p.m.; Saturday, noon to 11 p.m.; and Sunday, noon to 6 p.m.
Directions: Take US 95 north to the West Lake Mead Boulevard exit. Take West Lake Mead Boulevard to Tenaya Avenue. Laser Quest is on the corner of West Lake Mead and Tenaya.

This is big-time laser tag. Play 20-minute games in a 9,000-square-foot maze with a futuristic atmosphere created by theatrical fog, black lights, and florescent paint. Players wear a nine-pound vest with targets on it. If you shoot an opponent on one of the targets, you get a point; if you get shot, you lose a point. The facility can accommodate up to 30 people at a time. Children must be seven or older. Each game is $7, but memberships can reduce the rate. Package rates are available for large parties. This is the only laser-tag facility in town outside of the smaller versions in the Circus Circus Adventuredome and the New York-New York arcade.

Paintball Adventure

Battlefield
7400 Ronemus Drive

Pro Shop
3656 North Rancho Drive #102
702/647-0000
www.paintballadventurelv.com

Hours: Summer hours, Friday and Saturday, every other weekend, 7 p.m. to midnight. Winter hours, Saturday, 9 a.m. to 5 p.m. and Sunday, 10 a.m. to 5 p.m. The pro shop is open Tuesday through Friday from 3 to 8 p.m.
Directions: For the pro shop, take US 95 north to Craig Road. At the exit ramp, turn right. Take a right on Rancho Drive. The Pro Shop is on the left. For the battlefield, take US 95 north to Cheyenne Avenue. At the exit ramp, turn left. Take Cheyenne west past Tenaya. Turn left on Ronemus. The field is in the water retention basin. Enter through the softball park.

Know the joy of close-order combat without the injuries and fatalities. Refereed battles are held on weekend nights. Contestants divide into two teams and go at it with compressed-gas guns loaded with paintballs. If you get shot, you're out. Last team standing wins. Games last from five to 20 minutes. Children as young as 10 are welcome to play. For $20 per day (or night), you get field admission and rental of a uniform, facemask, gun, and unlimited CO_2 to power the gun. Paintballs are extra and run $20 for 500 shots to $60 for 2,000 shots. The equipment and paint are available at the field. You don't need to go to the pro shop unless you want to buy equipment. There's no food or drink available at the field. It's recommended you bring your own snacks and beverages, and don't forget water. No alcoholic beverages allowed.

Powerhouse Indoor Climbing Center

8201 West Charleston Avenue
702/254-5604
Hours: Monday through Thursday, 11 a.m. to 10 p.m.; Friday, 11 a.m. to 8 p.m.; Saturday and Sunday, 10 a.m. to 8 p.m.
Directions: Take Las Vegas Boulevard north to Charleston Avenue; turn left. Take Charleston west past Buffalo Road.

This indoor climbing gym is a great place to burn off some excess energy. Climbers of all skill levels can practice on an 8,000-square-foot 35-foot-high climbing wall. Day passes start at $10 for the bouldering option to climb without ropes. For $22 you can rent ropes and harnesses and do some serious climbing. Separately, day passes are $14 and shoes and equipment rental are $8. No one under 12 is allowed to climb without a parent, but there's no age limit if parents are along.

Nevada Climbing Centers

3065 East Patrick Lane, Suite 4

702/898-8192

www.nevadaclimbingcenters.com (under construction at press time)

Hours: Monday, Wednesday, and Friday, 11 a.m. to 10 p.m.; Tuesday and Thursday, 6 a.m. to 10 p.m.; Saturday, 11 a.m. to midnight; and Sunday 11 a.m. to 9 p.m.

Directions: Take Las Vegas Boulevard south to Sunset Road; turn left. Take Sunset Road to Eastern Avenue; turn left. Take Eastern Avenue to Patrick Lane; turn right. Nevada Climbing Centers is in an industrial complex on the right side of Patrick Lane.

This indoor facility allows you to try out the extreme sport of rock climbing in a safe atmosphere and provides guided hikes and tours to try out your skills. You can practice and take lessons on 14,000 square feet of simulated rock walls that go up to 30 feet high. Day passes for the climbing center are $12 and multi-pass specials and membership rates are available. Climbing shoes, harnesses, and other equipment are available for rent. A full rental package is $8 and includes full-body harnesses for the little one. Helmets are free. There's no age limit for the indoor facility. Instruction starts at $100 for group half-day lessons. Check out the Web page for more information on hikes, tours, and discovery programs for beginners to advanced climbers.

Sport Center

121 East Sunset Road
702/317-7777
www.sportcenterlasvegas.com
Hours: Friday, 4 p.m. to 8 p.m.; Saturday and Sunday, noon to 8 p.m.
Directions: Take Las Vegas Boulevard south to Sunset Road; turn left. The Sport Center is on the left.

The Sport Center's main business focuses on conventions, groups, and parties, but the Go-Kart Speed Park and Slugger Stadium batting cages are open to the public. The go-karts are $5 per ride or $20 for five. You must be at least 51 inches tall to drive and at least 36 inches tall to ride along. Passenger tickets are $3. Batting tokens for the Slugger Stadium start at $2 for 20 pitches. The cages are available for rent by the hour. Batting lessons are also offered.

Dansey's Indoor R/C Hobbies

741 North Nellis Boulevard
702/453-7223
www.danseys.com
Hours: The hobby shop is open daily from 10 a.m. to 9 p.m.; tracks open at 3 p.m.; closed Monday and Tuesday.
Directions: Take Flamingo Road east to Nellis Boulevard. Turn left. Dansey's is on the left past Bonanza Road.

This is the local ROAR (Remotely Operated Auto Racers) facility. ROAR members can participate in daily races on an outdoor off-road track or an indoor paved track. Between races, non-members can use the tracks for practice with their own cars or with rentals. Track use is $5 per day, rentals start at $8 per half-hour plus $5 for insurance. ROAR memberships are also available. There aren't any age limits, but the folks at Dansey's

Dansey's Indoor R/C Hobbie racetrack, courtesy Dansey's

say that children under eight or so probably won't have the coordination to really enjoy the experience. Dansey's is also a hobby shop with everything from dollhouses to scooters. You could spend quite a while just window shopping.

Steve-N-Kids Clubhouse

276 South Decatur Boulevard
702/434-5235
Hours: Monday through Friday, 9 a.m. to 5 p.m.
Directions: Take US 95 north; exit at Decatur. Steve's Clubhouse is on the northwest corner of Decatur and Meadows Lane, next to Target.

At last, something especially for the little ones (my people, as I like to call them). Steve-N-Kids Clubhouse is a playroom for children under six. This converted storefront has a jump house, sand box, scooters, dress-up costumes, blocks, toy cars, hobby horses, games, books, and more—all with the little kids in mind. The business is geared toward parties, but daily admission is $6 per child, and adults and children under one are free. Parents must be present; this isn't a babysitting service. Steve's is a great place for tots to let off some steam on a hot summer afternoon.

Clark County pool, courtesy Clark County Parks and Community Services

Public Parks and Pools

Las Vegas sports dozens of public parks, several public pools, and water parks with slides, wading pools, and fountains. Most of the public facilities are under the auspices of either Clark County Parks and Community Services or Las Vegas Leisure Services. Both have Web sites with addresses and phone numbers, but the Clark County site is easier to use and provides more detail. On the Las Vegas site, you can search by the activity you're interested in. Almost all the parks have playgrounds, but not all have restrooms. Why in the world they'd build a playground with no restroom I've never understood. Be sure to check on the available facilities before heading out.

Clark County Parks and Community Services

702/455-8200

www.co.clark.nv.us/parks/homepage.htm

City of Las Vegas Leisure Services

702/229-6297

www.lasvegasnevada.gov/leisure_services

Following is information on some of the larger parks.

Sunset Park

2601 Sunset Road

702/455-8200

Directions: Take Las Vegas Boulevard south to Sunset Road; turn left. Take Sunset past the airport to Eastern Avenue. The park is on the right on the southeast corner of Sunset and Eastern.

Hours: Daily, 7 a.m. to 11 p.m.

This may be one of the only public parks in the world with a neon sign at the entrance. Sunset Park is one of the largest and oldest parks in the valley. The county has reserved more than 350 acres, but only 150 are developed. The trees are old and large, so there's lots of shade and huge swaths of grass. There's even a lake stocked for fishing. You'll find baseball fields, basketball, tennis, volleyball and horseshoe courts, playgrounds, picnic areas, a dog park, a fitness court, and a multitude of trees. There's also a public pool. Wildlife such as rabbits, chipmunks, and quail might be spotted in some of the less populated sections. The area is also known for bird viewing.

Desert Breeze Park

8425 Spring Mountain Road
702/455-8334
Hours: Daily, 7 a.m. to 11 p.m.
Directions: From the Las Vegas Strip, take Spring Mountain Road west past Fort Apache Road to Durango Drive.

This is one of the newer large parks in the area, so the equipment is shiny and new, but the landscaping is sparse. There's lots of grass and some of the playgrounds are covered to provide some shade in the summer, but the trees need time to grow. Still, you can't beat this place for facilities. There are baseball fields, indoor and outdoor basketball courts, a dog park, a skate park, and a walking trail. There is also an indoor pool and an outdoor water play area with slides, fountains, and a wading pool.

Lorenzi Park

3333 West Washington Avenue
702/229-6704
Hours: Daily, 8 a.m. to 10 p.m.
Directions: Take US 95 north to Rancho Drive; turn right. Take Rancho to Washington Avenue; turn left. The park is on the left.

One of the oldest parks in the city, this park has mature landscaping with huge trees and lots of shaded picnic areas, but the grand old lady is a little ragged around the edges. Once known as Twin Lakes, there is only one lake now. You can fish for bluegill or feed the ducks and other waterfowl. This park is the home of the local rose club's garden, the Nevada State Historical Museum, the Las Vegas Art Museum, and the Sammy Davis, Junior outdoor festival plaza. You'll find tennis courts, baseball fields, soccer fields, basketball courts, shuffleboard, and playgrounds.

There's a fitness course and a wheelchair fitness court, plus a small garden for the blind. The park is located near the center of the city. It's a nice getaway in the daytime, but tends to be taken over by rougher elements later in the evening.

Floyd Lamb State Park

9200 Tule Springs Road
702/486-5413
Hours: Daily, 8 a.m. to 8 p.m.
Directions: Take US 95 north to Durango Road; turn right. Follow the signs to Tule Springs Road.

This might be the only park in the world named after a convicted felon. Nevadans learned a valuable lesson about naming things after living people when State Senator Floyd Lamb went to prison in a bribery scandal. This park evolved from a dude ranch built in the 1940s called Tule Springs (many locals still call the park by that name). The ranch was built as a divorce retreat where the soon-to-be-unmarried would wait out their six-week residencies. Some of the stables and other buildings still stand. You'll find four stocked lakes and trails for walking and biking. Huge cottonwood trees shade lovely picnic areas. Not long ago, this was a remote spot from the city. Now it's surrounded by development. Admission is $5 per car.

4
Jaunts and Day Trips

The very best parts of Southern Nevada lie beyond the urban sprawl of the Las Vegas Valley. This chapter focuses on adventures located a good day trip away from the Las Vegas Strip. Experience something completely different and still be back at your hotel or safely at home by nightfall. It's the best of both worlds.

Cowboy Experience

Real cowboys aren't the gun-toting tough guys seen in the John Wayne movies. They never were. Indians, or Native Americans as they now prefer to be called, are neither the vicious warriors nor the noble savages depicted in fiction. They never were. Early cowboys were youngsters hired to drive cattle out to forage during the day and back to their barns at night. Real Indians were primitive people trying to survive in a harsh environment and maintain their lifestyle in a quickly changing world. In rural Southern Nevada, visitors get to have it both ways. At one stop, you can experience the classic Wild West of the movies, then, just down the road, see what life in the Old West was really like. Enjoy it all, but try to keep fantasy and reality separated.

Bonnie Springs Old Nevada

Nevada Highway 159
702/875-4191
www.bonniesprings.com
Hours: Summer hours, 10:30 a.m. to 6 p.m.; winter hours, 10:30 a.m. to 5 p.m.
Directions: Take US 95 north to Summerlin Parkway. Take the parkway to I-215 and turn left (south). Exit I-215 at Charleston Boulevard and turn right. Bonnie Springs is about nine miles on the right. Shuttle service from Las Vegas is available. Call Star Land Tours at 702/296-4381.

I've been taking children to Bonnie Springs for 30 years and they still love it. Although it's a shoddy rundown tourist trap in my opinion, kids see it through different eyes. There are two distinct sections. One is the Old Nevada area with a petting zoo, riding stables, and a quaint old restaurant and bar. A man-made pond stocked with rather aggressive ducks and swans is in front of the restaurant. Then there's the Western Town with gift shops, saloon, etc., where gunfights and melodramas are staged regularly during the day. In the old days, we never went into the Western Town. They charged admission and it was never worth the price. The kids liked the free petting zoo better anyway. Things have changed. Now there's an admission fee of $5 on weekdays and $10 on weekends per car just to park and both the petting zoo and the Old Western

Bonnie Springs, courtesy Las Vegas Convention and Vistor's Authority

town are included in the price. A kiddie train runs from a remote parking lot to the entrance on weekends. This is the only place I know of in the Las Vegas area where you can see a live buffalo. The petting zoo, which has always seemed rather smelly and slapdash to me, has goats, deer, and llamas. Local and exotic animals are held in cages and there are your requisite peacocks and chickens. My granddaughter got a big kick out of meeting Bambi in person.

Bruno's Indian Museum

1306 Nevada Highway
Boulder City
702/293-4865
Hours: Daily, 10 a.m. to 5 p.m.
Directions: Take US 93 to Hoover Dam. Bruno's is located at the dam.

They call it a museum, but Bruno's is mostly a Native American gift shop, jewelry store, and art gallery that claims to educate the public about the Native American artists of the Southwest. They say 2,000 artists are represented in the fine-art gallery and jewelry store. Worth stopping in while you are at the dam.

Spring Mountain Ranch State Park

8000 West Blue Diamond Road
Blue Diamond
702/875-4141
http://parks.nv.gov/smr.htm
Hours: The main ranch house is open daily from 10 a.m. to 4 p.m. Guided tours are available weekdays at noon, 1 p.m., and 2 p.m., and on weekends at noon, 1 p.m., 2 p.m., and 3 p.m. The picnic area is open daily from 8 a.m. until dusk.
Directions: Head west on Charleston Boulevard (it soon be-

comes Nevada Highway 159) and keep going for 15 miles. After you pass Red Rock Canyon National Park, Spring Mountain Ranch is on the right. Or take US 95 north to Summerlin Parkway. Take the parkway to I-215 and turn left (south). Exit I-215 at Charleston Boulevard and turn right. The ranch is about eight miles on the right.

At the base of the magnificent Wilson Cliffs to the west of Las Vegas lies Spring Mountain Ranch. This 520-acre oasis was developed into a combination working ranch and luxurious retreat by a string of owners, including Howard Hughes and Vera Krupp, who also owned the Krupp diamond. Amazingly, those two are probably not the most colorful inhabitants. The ranch's history goes back to the mid-1830s when the spring-fed creek and meadow provided a refreshing oasis on the Spanish Trail. Outlaws, mountain men, horse thieves, and Indian slave traders were once known to hide out at the site. Today, visitors can enjoy guided tours of the ranch house and historic outbuildings. The ranch is also a great spot for picnicking and hiking. The park also sports an outdoor pavilion where plays and musicals are performed in the summer. Admission is $5 per car.

Spring Mountain Ranch, courtesy Spring Mountain Ranch

Cowboy Trail Rides, courtesy Las Vegas Convention and Vistor's Authority

Cowboy Trail Rides

Nevada Highway 159
702/948-7061
www.cowboytrailrides.com
Hours: By appointment.
Directions: Take Charleston Boulevard west into Red Rock Canyon. Stables are on the left, across from the entrance to the Red Rock Conservation Area. Or take US 95 north to Summerlin Parkway. Take the parkway to I-215 and turn left (south). Exit I-215 at Charleston Boulevard and turn right. The stables are on the left.

This service offers guided trail rides to ridges with a spectacular view of Red Rock Canyon and the surrounding mountains. A 1½-hour ride runs $69 and a 2-hour ride is $89. A sunset ride followed by a Western barbecue back at the stables is $139 per person. The staff is friendly and the horses seem well-trained and cared for. This is a great way to get out and see what the desert really looks like. The trail rides are open only to children tall enough to reach the stirrups. They don't advertise it, but if you ask, they'll do a short pony ride for little kids for $10.

Mount Charleston Riding Stables
Mount Charleston
702/872-5408
www.mtcharlestonlodge.com
Hours: Daily 9 a.m. to 6 p.m.
Directions: Take US 95 north to Kyle Canyon Road. Turn left. The stables are just below the Mt. Charleston Hotel on the right.

In warm weather, you can enjoy the cool of the 5,000- to 8,000-foot elevation of Mt. Charleston by horseback. Guided rides run $30 per hour and you can arrange rides from one hour to several if you have the energy. Several different trails start just below the lodge. Trail rides are only for children whose feet can reach the stirrups. For younger children and groups, carriage rides are $10 for adults and $5 for children under 12. In the winter, when snow usually covers the ground, horse-drawn sleigh rides are available. The cost is $10 for adults and $7 for children. End your winter ride with hot chocolate in the old Mount Charleston Lodge. If you ask, wranglers will arrange a pony ride for little kids for $10 for about 15 to 20 minutes.

Ride Easy, Ride Hard

Do you like heart-stopping death-defying adventure or do you prefer your thrills of a more laid-back variety? Following are options for varying tastes.

Desert Princess Cruise

Lake Mead Cruises
480 Lake Shore Drive
Boulder City
702/293-6180
www.lakemeadcruises.com
Hours: Vary
Directions: Take I-215 East to US 93 South to Boulder City. Follow the signs to Lake Mead Marina.

Take a cruise on Lake Mead in a replica riverboat paddle wheeler. The boat has two indoor decks and one outdoor upper deck, so cruises are enjoyable all year round. The cruise includes an unusual look at the top side of Hoover Dam. The food served on the breakfast and dinner cruises is so-so, but the exciting atmosphere more than makes up for it. The Breakfast Buffet Cruise runs on Sundays from April through October for a cost of $28.50 for adults and $15 for children. The Mid-Day Sightseeing Cruise includes no food

Desert Princess Cruise, courtesy Las Vegas Convention and Vistor's Authority

and costs $19 for adults and $9 for children. The Early Dinner Cruise includes a set dinner menu of beef, chicken, seafood, or pasta. These cruises are $39.50 per adult and $21 per child. The Dinner Dance Cruise, which includes cocktails and dancing, goes for $51 per adult and is not recommended for children. Times vary with the season, so call ahead.

Desperado Roller Coaster and Turbo Drop

Buffalo Bill's Resort and Casino
Primm
800-367-7383
www.primmvalleygolfclub.com
Hours: Monday and Thursday, noon to 6 p.m.; Friday, 11 a.m. to midnight; Saturday, 10 a.m. to midnight; and Sunday, 10 a.m. to 7 p.m.
Directions: Take I-15 south. Buffalo Bill's is 35 miles on the left.

This is billed as the country's tallest and fastest roller coaster. It is also the one with the longest drop: 225 feet. The height itself is scary enough, but the drop goes into an underground tunnel, making it even more frightening. Or so I'm told. You'll never get me on the thing. They say it goes from 80 to 90 miles per hour over 6,000 feet of track. You board inside the hotel and travel out of and around it. People come from all over the world to ride this coaster. I've seen kids who were positively green after the experience, yet ready to go again. Go figure.

Buffalo Bill's also has a flume ride, a motion simulator, and a thing called the Turbo Drop, sort of an upside down Big Shot (Stratosphere). These are all located in an extensive arcade. Children must be 48 inches tall to ride the Desperado and 46 inches to ride the Turbo Drop, but there are other rides suitable for younger children. The roller coaster costs $7 per ride and the Turbo Drop is $5.

Desperado Roller Coaster, courtesy MGM Mirage

Bonnie & Clyde "Ambush Car"
Whiskey Pete's Hotel & Casino
Primm
www.primmvalleygolfclub.com
Hours: 24 hours.
Directions: Take I-15 south. Whiskey Pete's is about 35 miles on the right.

Here's a gruesome one for you. While you're in Primm to ride the Desperado, see the actual bullet-riddled Ford that notorious thugs Bonnie and Clyde died in. It used to be known as the Bonnie and Clyde Death Car, but when the hotel was taken over by the MGM Mirage Corp., the PR machine decided "death" was too harsh. Other artifacts on display include a letter from the Ford Motor Company authenticating the car and a letter from Clyde Barrow to Ford singing the praises of the vehicle as a get-away car. Recently added is the blood-stained shirt Clyde was wearing when he was killed by the FBI. This is not my idea of wholesome entertainment, but your kids might get a kick out of it.

Bonnie & Clyde "Ambush Car," courtesy MGM Mirage

Great Outdoor Adventures

Camping, boating, off-roading, hiking; we've got it all. Spend a short time driving and a lot of time enjoying some of the most spectacular scenery in the world. Take it easy or test your endurance with a rugged mountain hike. There's something here for everyone.

Lake Mead Marina, courtesy Las Vegas Convention and Vistor's Authority

Lake Mead National Recreation Area

601 Nevada Highway
Boulder City
702/293-8907
702/293-8990
www.nps.gov/lame
Directions: There are several ways to get to Lake Mead. One is to take I-215 to US 93/95 and turn right toward Boulder City. Follow the signs to the Lake Mead Marina. Or turn left off of US 93/95 at Lake Mead Drive in Henderson and follow the signs to North Shore Road.

My favorite place on Lake Mead is one you could never find in a million years.

Lake Mead was created by Hoover Dam and is the largest man-made lake in the nation, with 181,000 acres of water and almost 1,000 miles of shoreline. Unfortunately, most of the spots accessible by land are littered with trash left behind by the ignorant and thoughtless. Therefore, the most pristine coves and beaches are accessible only by boat or jet ski. Boating is indeed a popular lake activity, so popular in fact that the traffic on the water can be terrific on summer holiday weekends. Fishing is also popular. The lake offers large-mouth bass, striped bass, catfish, rainbow trout, sunfish, crappie, and bluegill. It's also a great place to camp, picnic, and swim if you pick your spot carefully.

The recreation area also includes Lake Mohave to the south. That area is cleaner but has fewer services and is harder to get

to. One of my favorite spots on Lake Mohave is Cottonwood Cove. To get there, take US 93 toward Boulder City and turn right just after you pass the Railroad Pass. Take US 95 south 36 miles to Searchlight. Turn left and travel 14 miles east to Cottonwood Cove. There

Lake Mead, courtesy Nevada Commission on Tourism

you'll find a beach, campground, boat landing, marina, and motel. There are also some nice hiking trails that wind over the sandstone rocks and along the shoreline.

Lake Mead also offers several marinas and beaches. Another favorite is Echo Bay off of North Shore Road, with a marina, motel, and a nice little restaurant.

Some people like to grab a map and take off exploring (I recommend the *Nevada Atlas and Gazetteer* by DeLorme, available in most bookstores). If that's your pleasure, be careful. A long-term drought in the West has reduced the water level in the lake dramatically. Land that was under water for decades is now exposed. The top layers of soil have dried out in some places, so it looks like good solid land, but underneath is a knee-deep bog. Watch where you drive or walk.

Take safety precautions seriously. We lose several people a year at the lake.

The Alan Bible Visitor Center off US 93 near Boulder City is a good place to get maps and find out about conditions. Information stations are located at Overton Beach, Echo Bay, Callville Bay, and Las Vegas Bay.

The entrance fee for the recreation area is $5 per car for five days.

Valley of Fire State Park

Overton
702/397-2088
http://parks.nv.gov/vf.htm
Hours: Visitor Center is open daily from 8:30 a.m. to 4:30 p.m.
Directions: Take I-15 north to Nevada Highway 169 (Exit 75); turn right. Follow the signs to Valley of Fire.

The landscape in Valley of Fire is so out-of-this-world it was used as a set in "Star Trek: Generations." The valley is named for the red sandstone formations carved out by millions of years of sand erosion. See ancient trees that are now pieces of petrified wood and petroglyphs, rocks etched by Indians 3,000 years ago. This is a great place for camping, hiking, picnicking, and photography. The scenery is incredible any time, but after a rainy winter, the wildflowers come out to provide a breathtaking experience in the spring. There's lots of wildlife and great examples of desert flora. You might get lucky and see a bighorn sheep. The park offers a full-scale visitor center with extensive interpretive displays. Several group-use areas are also available. Camp sites have tables, grills, and water, and restrooms are nearby. A dump station for RVs and showers are also available. The park is open and accessible all year. The entrance fee is $5 per car. The cost to enter and camp is $13 per car.

Valley of Fire (top), courtesy Las Vegas Convention and Vistor's Authority

Red Rock Canyon (center) and Burros just off Highway 159 (right), courtesy Nevada Commission on Toursim

Red Rock Canyon
    Nevada Highway 159
    702/515-5350
    www.redrockcanyon.blm.gov
    Hours: Visitors' Center is open daily from 8 a.m. to 5:30 p.m.
    The scenic drive is open daily from 6 a.m. to 8 p.m.
    Directions: Located 18 miles west of the Strip. Head west on
    Charleston Boulevard.

Red Rock Canyon's close proximity to Las Vegas is one of its benefits and one of its detriments. Its red sandstone cliffs are popular with tourists, but the area has become so crowded that many locals no longer go there. The canyon is a National Conservation Area managed by the Bureau of Land Management. It covers 197,000 acres of hiking trails, picnic areas, camp sites, and scenic overlooks. The one-way 13-mile scenic drive starts and ends at Highway 159. The visitors' center features exhibits on the geology, topography, and plant and animal life of the area. Rangers conduct tours and educational programs. The canyon is popular with rock climbers and mountaineers. People come from all over to scale the cliffs and rock formations. Some of the scenic overlooks offer a great view of climbers high on the cliff walls. The entrance fee is $5 per car or $20 for an annual pass. There is no charge for walkers or bicyclists.

The area has one campground located two miles east of the visitors' center on the other side of Nevada Highway 159. It is a dry camp with no water, no electricity, no shade—not much of anything, really. There are faucets for drinking water available and pit toilets. Camping is $10 per night or $25 for groups.

Mount Charleston

702/872-0156

Directions: Take US 93 north to Kyle Canyon Road; turn left. The turnoff to Lee Canyon is 10 miles ahead.

Mt. Charleston hike, courtesy Las Vegas Convention and Vistor's Authority

Mount Charleston is the highest mountain in the Spring Mountain range to the west and northwest of the Las Vegas Valley. The area is part of the Humbolt-Toiyabe National Forest and is managed by the U.S. Forest Service and the Bureau of Land Management. For generations, Las Vegans have used Mount Charleston as an escape from the summer heat. The small residential area that now occupies the Kyle Canyon side of the mountain was founded by early gaming execs who built mountain retreats there for their families. Long before that, the Paiute Indians took refuge on the mountain in the warm weather and retreated to lower points in winter.

At its highest point, Charleston Peak towers 11,900 feet above the Las Vegas Valley at about 2,100 feet. The differences in temperature and landscape are astounding. Huge Ponderosa pine trees create a shady canopy and give the air an incredible fragrance. Wildflowers, birds, and animals thrive. Average high temperatures hover in the 80s in the summertime.

There are two main areas open and readily accessible to the public. Kyle Canyon is the closest to Las Vegas. This is where the residential area is. It is also the location of the Mount Charleston Hotel, a relatively new facility that sits outside the recreation area, and the Mount Charleston Lodge, a 40-plus-year-old mountain lodge higher up on the paved road.

Lee Canyon, found farther up US 95, is smaller and less populated. There are no residences and the only commercial enterprise is the Lee Canyon Ski Area.

The area offers many outdoor activities in the summer and is where Las Vegas children go to learn about snow in the winter. Discussed below are some of the more popular activities.

Hiking

There's something for everyone in the way of hiking, from the easy 850-yard hike to Robber's Roost to the back-breaking 10-mile trek to Charleston Peak on the North Loop. The Bristlecone Trail off Lee Canyon Road (Nevada Highway 156) leads to a forest of bristlecone pines, the world's oldest living trees.

Hikers should arm themselves with plenty of water, sunscreen, and a map. The Forest Service provides a helpful brochure. Guidebooks and map books are

Bristlecone Trail, courtesy Nevada Commission on Tourism

available at outdoor supply stores and the local bookstores. *Hiking Las Vegas* by Branch Whitney is highly recommended to the serious hiker.

Camping and Picnicking

Campgrounds and picnic areas abound on the mountain. Some have showers and some are handicap accessible. There's even an RV camp site, but it has no water or toilet facilities. The camp sites are popular so it's hard to find a spot. It is highly recommended that reservations be made in advance by calling the National Reservation Center at 877-444-6777. Camp fees run from $14 per night for single family units to $70 per night for the RV park. Multi-family and large group sites are also available.

My family has always avoided the developed camp sites. We prefer to camp in privacy and make do without showers and toilets. If that is your pleasure, find a dirt road and follow it until the scenery is to your liking (see the *Nevada Atlas and Gazetteer* by DeLorme). Always try to find a spot that has been used before so you'll disturb the habitat as little as possible. Campfires are permitted most of the time, except during extreme drought conditions. Please be mindful of the rules and warnings and, for heaven sake, take your trash out with you. The rule at our house is that we always try to take out a little more trash than we take in. If everyone did that, just think how lovely and pristine your forests would be.

Skiing

Lee Canyon Ski and Snowboard Resort

702/645-2754
www.skilasvegas.com
Hours: 9 a.m. to 4 p.m., weather permitting.
Directions: Take US 95 north to the Lee Canyon turnoff. The resort is at the end of the paved road, Highway 156.

Imagine being able to ski just an hour's drive from Las Vegas. The Lee Canyon Ski and Snowboard Resort isn't exactly Vail, Colorado, but to us desert rats it can be snow heaven. Resort management says they like to think the slopes will be open from Thanksgiving to Easter, but most years that's a pipe dream. Even the snowmaking equipment can't compensate for high temperatures. When it's open and the conditions are just right, Lee Canyon can be a great place to ski. I learned how to ski there and so did my kids. There are 10 trails that start at 8,500 feet and go up to 9,500. The three lifts include one on the bunny slope. The lodge offers so-so food at high prices and equipment is available for rent.

We stopped going to Lee Canyon years ago because it was just too crowded. An additional lift and more trails have been added since then, but the population pressure from the valley persists. There is one day of the year you can ski without long lines and mobs of snowboarders: Super Bowl Sunday. The lifts close at 4 p.m., just about half-time. You can head to the lodge and watch the last half of the game (if you must).

Snow Play

Mt. Charleston is where local children are introduced to the wonders of snow. I've spent many a glorious afternoon on Mt. Charleston with untold numbers of children. Sledding is the great attraction for kids large and small. We always end up trying to build a snowman, but it never works out. The snow in the high desert is extremely dry. There's hardly enough moisture in it to make a decent snowball, much less the snow boulders required for a good snowman or -woman. But that never stops us from trying. When there's adequate snow on the ground, the picnic and snow play areas are packed, especially on the weekend. Take dry wood to build a fire, a thermos of hot drinks, and lots of dry clothes. The beauty of playing in the snow on Mt. Charleston is that when the kids get cold and cranky you can throw them in the car, head back to the valley, and leave the snow behind. You never have to shovel it or scrape it off your windshield before driving to work.

Ash Meadows National Wildlife Refuge
Amargosa Valley
775/372-5435
http://desertcomplex.fws.gov
Hours: Sunrise to sunset.
Directions: Take US 95 north to State Route 373. At Amargosa Junction, turn left (south). Travel 15 miles to Spring Meadows Road, turn left (east), and travel five miles to refuge headquarters.

Located about 90 miles north of Las Vegas, this natural oasis consists of 22,000 acres of spring-fed wetlands and alkaline desert uplands. Here, you can see 20 plants and animals found nowhere else in the world, but you have to look carefully. Most of them are pretty small, such as the Devil's Hole pupfish and the Ash Meadows speckled dace. See environmental extremes from sand dunes and ash tree groves to wetlands. It's a great place for bird and wildlife watching, picnicking, and even some swimming, fishing, and motorless boating in Crystal Reservoir. In another area, a boardwalk takes you through a wetlands conservation area to Crystal Springs and several informational signs describe the plant and animal life around you. At the northeast corner of the refuge is Devil's Hole, actually part of Death Valley, a flooded cave entrance that is the last remaining habitat for the endangered Devil's Hole pupfish. The hole is not much to look at, hard to find, and surrounded by a big fence to protect the pupfish.

Facilities such as restrooms, water fountains, and picnic tables are available but scarce. Be sure to take food and plenty of water. This is an interesting stop off on the way to or from Death Valley, but not really worth a trip in itself.

Ash Meadows National Wildlife Refuge, photo by Kathy Espin

History on Display

Kyle Ranch

Carey Avenue and Losee Road
North Las Vegas
http://dmla.clan.lib.nv.us/docs/shpo/markers/mark_224.htm
Directions: Take I-15 north to Cheyenne Avenue. Turn left at the ramp and go across the overpass. Turn left on Losee Road. The ranch is located at Carey and Losee roads in North Las Vegas.

The ranch was established by Conrad Kiel in 1875 and was one of only two major ranches in the Las Vegas Valley throughout the 19th century. The ranch has a violent history. Neighboring rancher Archibald Stewart was killed in a gunfight here in 1884 over the honor of Stewart's wife, Helen, known as the First Lady of Las Vegas. Edwin and William Kiel were found murdered on the ranch in October 1900. Remains of the ranch include an unassuming stone and wood ranch house and a white shed that date back to the glory days of the ranch. There is no admission fee.

Lost City Museum of Archaeology

721 South Moapa Valley Boulevard
Overton
702/397-2193
Hours: Daily, 8:30 a.m. to 4:30 p.m., except Thanksgiving, Christmas, and New Year's Day.
Directions: Take I-15 north about 45 miles to Nevada Highway 169. Take 169 right through Logandale to Overton. Just past Overton, the museum is on the right (west) side of the road.

The Lost City Museum was established by the National Park Service to exhibit artifacts excavated from Pueblo Grande de

Nevada, a 30-mile-long settlement colonized by the Anasazi Indians from the first to the 12th century AD. In the 1930s, after Hoover Dam was built, the waters of Lake Mead began inundating many of the

Lost City Museum, courtesy Nevada Commission on Tourism

ancient sites. With the help of the Civilian Conservation Corporation, artifacts were excavated to save them from being lost forever. The museum contains a reconstruction of an Anasazi pueblo house that is built on the original foundation from centuries ago. There's also a reconstruction of a pithouse that once belonged to Basketmaker Indians (ancestors of today's Paiutes) who moved in after the Anasazi left. There is a notable collection of Native American pottery, arrowheads, and other artifacts. The museum is currently owned and maintained by the State of Nevada. Programs include ongoing archaeological research on the remaining Lost City sites, school tours and outreach programs,

changing exhibits, and an archival library for research. Admission is $2 for adults 18 and over. Children 17 and under are free.

Lost City Museum, courtesy Lost City Museum

Nevada Test Site Tour & Atomic Testing Museum

Mercury
775 East Flamingo Road
Las Vegas
702/794-5161
www.nv.doe.gov
Directions: From the Strip, take Flamingo Road east past Swensen. The museum, which is the departure point for the tour, is inside the Desert Research Institute building on the right.

This may seem like a strange way to spend a day, but science and history buffs find this tour of the nuclear test site fascinating. Founded in 1951, the test site is about 65 miles north of Las Vegas. This huge "outdoor laboratory" is bigger than Rhode Island. From 1951 to 1992, the test site was ground zero for 928 above- and belowground nuclear tests. Bombs were dropped from planes, detonated on towers, from balloons, and in tunnels. The mushroom clouds from aboveground tests could be seen from Las Vegas. The tour includes some artifacts and archaeological sites from early settlers and relics from the nuclear weapons tests, rocket experiments, and astronaut training conducted over the years. The tours are offered once a

Test bomb, courtesy Nevada Commission on Tourism

month except during the hot summer months and leave Las Vegas at 7 a.m. returning about 4 p.m. No food is provided, so be sure to pack a lunch, but don't take cameras, tape recorders, or cell phones. Security is serious. You must make reservations at least two to three weeks in advance to allow time for security clearance. No children under 14 are allowed to participate and it is recommended that pregnant women skip this tour, not because of potential exposure to radiation but because of the long bus ride and the rough terrain. Check the DOE Web site for dates.

Science buffs who don't have time or energy to take the tour will certainly want to check out the new museum. There are lots of video displays of historical events that put the events at the test site into perspective. The Ground Zero Theater, designed like the concrete bunkers used at the test site, shows video of an actual above-ground detonation. There are tons of photos and other artifacts including accounts from former employees and thousands of declassified documents. The museum is open Monday through Saturday, 9 a.m. to 5 p.m. and Sunday, 1 p.m. to 5 p.m.; admission is $10 with discounts for seniors, students, and military.

Hoover Dam

US 95
Nevada/Arizona Border
702/597-5970
www.usbr.gov/lc/hooverdam/
Hours: Parking Garage, 8 a.m. to 6 p.m.; Visitor Center, 9 a.m. to 5 p.m.
Directions: Head south on US 93/95 through Boulder City. You can't miss it.

The Bureau of Reclamation has been conducting tours of Hoover Dam since it opened in 1937. The thousands of men who came to work on the dam during the Great Depression helped give Las Vegas its start as an entertainment mecca. For almost 70 years the dam has been generating electricity for Southern California and other parts of the Southwest. It also helps control the flow of the Colorado River. Before the dam was built, the river tended to flood or dry up, making life uncertain for people dependent on it as a source of water. Lake Mead, the huge reservoir created by the dam, now provides water to California, Nevada, New Mexico, Utah, Arizona, and Mexico. The dam is a National Historic Landmark and has been rated by the American Society of Civil Engineers as one of America's Seven Modern Civil Engineering Wonders.

The dam was just one of many public works endeavors instigated by the Hoover Administration to stimulate the economy and create jobs for displaced workers. It was destined to be a showpiece of American workmanship. Its showy art-deco de-

Hoover Dam river raft tour, courtesy Las Vegas Convention and Visitor's Authority

sign—hardly utilitarian—seems out of place for a power plant.

Until the terrorist attacks of 2001, the Bureau of Reclamation offered a variety of tours, some of which took visitors deep into the workings of the dam. I was once privileged to enjoy what was known as a "hard-hat" tour that provided a fascinating behind-the-scenes look at this engineering marvel. Today, Discovery tours have replaced both the traditional guided tours and the hard-hat tours. The new tour is self-paced with guides stationed at various locations in the visitor's center and on top of the dam. Visitors can take the elevators down into the dam to see the huge generators cranking out power, but interior access is limited for obvious security reasons. The visitors' center is an extensive museum dedicated to the history and engineering of the dam. It's too bad the old tours had to be discontinued, but the dam is still well worth the trip. Visit during Pacific Standard Time and you can have the fun of standing in two states and two time zones at the same time.

Boulder City Museum

1305 Arizona Street
Boulder City
702/294-1988
www.bcmha.org
Hours: Monday through Saturday, 10 a.m. to 5 p.m.; Sunday, noon to 5 p.m. Closed New's Year Day, Easter Sunday, Mother's Day, Thanksgiving, and Christmas Day.
Directions: Take US 93/95 south to Boulder City. Follow the signs to the museum.

This museum focuses more on the human history of the dam rather than the engineering feat described so well in the exhibits at the dam itself. Boulder City was founded as a federal enclave to house the dam workers and their families. The feds instituted a no-gambling and no-alcohol policy to protect the workforce from the wages of sin. Those founding principles still influence the city today. Prohibitions on alcohol have been lifted, but there is still no gambling in Boulder City; the nearest casino is Railroad Pass, several miles out of town. The city has also managed to hold on to the small-town atmosphere by placing strict limits on growth.

The museum, located on the ground floor of the historic Boulder Dam Hotel, tells the story of the hardships endured by those who came to build the dam. The interactive displays and exhibits go into the social forces that caused the Great Depression and made so many displaced workers available for construction jobs. Photographs and artifacts tell part of the story, but the oral histories of the workers and their families bring to life the sacrifice, danger, and hard work endured. The folks that run the museum and members of the Boulder City Museum and Historical Association are not likely to let us forget that the dam was originally known as Boulder Dam and they seem to have liked it better that way. The hotel, a large Colonial-style building, was completed in 1933 and attracted such movie stars as Bette Davis, Shirley Temple, Boris Karloff, and Will Rogers.

The museum is well worth a stop on the way to or from the dam. General admission is $2 and children and seniors pay $1.

5
Overnight Adventures

Want a real cultural experience? Dare to venture outside the Las Vegas Valley into the rural areas of Nevada, southern Utah, and western Arizona. Many of these trips can be made in a day, but it's more fun to spend at least one night where services are available. In many of these places, you will feel you have traveled back in time to at least the 1950s, when ovens were the conventional type and phones had dials. Now, that's roughing it.

Nevada

The sights and attractions in Nevada are arranged along two routes: one going north along US 95 and the other following US 93 off of I-15 north. Either way, take plenty of time to enjoy the wonders of rural Nevada.

Rhyolite Ghost Town
Nevada Highway 374
www.rhyolitesite.com
Directions: Take US 95 north to Beatty, Nevada (about 120 miles). Turn left on Nevada Highway 374 and follow the signs.

In 1904, when gold was discovered in the area, the town of

Rhyolite sprang up from the desert like so many mining boom-towns before it. Once a bustling town of 10,000, Rhyolite was named for the minerals found locally. At its peak, it had more than 50 saloons, 18 grocery stores, eight doctors, a half-dozen barbers, and 15 hotels. The heyday was short-lived. By 1911, the town was abandoned when financial backing for the mining operations collapsed. But Rhyolite was built to last, as you can see from the ruins left behind. Still standing are the train depot where three railroads once served the town, the two-story concrete school building, and the three-story frame of the Cook Bank Building. The most famous relic of Rhyolite is the Bottle House. It was built by Australian Thomas Kelly in 1905 of 51,000 glass bottles cemented together. It was one of three bottle houses built in Rhyolite, but the only one still intact. A volunteer camps out in an RV to protect the site and give visitors free guided tours. I believe it was Clint who greeted us on our last visit. I remember his jokes more than I do the facts he recited about the house and Rhyolite.

On the short road into Rhyolite off Nevada Highway 374 is an outdoor art exhibit with some interesting statuary, including a ghostly version of the Last Supper made of sheet-covered invisible figures.

Rhyolite is four miles west of Beatty near the entrance to Death Valley.

Goldfield

Goldfield
775/485-3560
www.ghosttowns.com/states/nv/goldfield.html
Directions: Take US 95 north past Beatty, (about 130 miles).

Goldfield was once the largest and most modern city in Nevada (though in 1902, that wasn't saying much). Shortly after gold was discovered, the population swelled to more than

Cook Bank building (above and right) and Rhyolite Last Supper ghost statues (below), courtesy Nevada Commission on Tourism

20,000 people. The town became known as the "Queen of Camps," with luxury seldom seen in mining towns. The mines produced $10,000 worth of ore per day that funded five banks and several mining stock exchanges. Three newspapers and five railroads served the town. Goldfield gained some national renown when a boxing match was staged between Joe Gans and Oscar Batling "Battlin" Nelson that went 42 rounds for a Guinness World Record. A flood in 1913 and a fire in 1923 destroyed many of the buildings, but a number of them still stand, including an old high school, the telephone building, and the regal-looking courthouse. Another must-see is the Goldfield Hotel, which is rumored to be haunted. The few hardy souls who still inhabit Goldfield are constantly wishing for a revival of the town. The latest hopes are pinned on a new owner who says he plans to restore the hotel. Many have tried before and failed. Goldfield is between Beatty and Tonopah and makes a nice stop when traveling between.

Central Nevada Museum

1900 Logan Field Road
Tonopah
775/482-9676
www.tonopahnevada.com/centralnevadamuseum.html
Hours: Wednesday through Sunday, 10 a.m. to 5 p.m. Closed from 1 to 2 p.m. for lunch, most federal holidays, and Nevada Day (October 31).
Directions: Take US 95 north to Tonopah (about 200 miles). Turn left on Logan Field Road. The museum is visible from US 95.

This is my favorite Nevada history museum. Inside are displays dedicated to the Native Americans who populated the area long before Europeans ever found the place, the mining that gave the town its start, and Army and Air Force facilities

Central Nevada
Museum (right and
below), photos by
Kathy Espin

that kept it going. There's a "playhouse" where children can experience home life of the early 1900s and there are displays of the local wildlife. Outside, however, is the best part: an incredible collection of early mining and construction equipment boggles the mind with its combination of simplicity, complexity, and ingenuity. From original early railroad tracks to a two-story-tall stamp mill, the collection seems endless. A collection of early buildings and dwellings has been carefully preserved and reconstructed in a way that gives you the feeling of authenticity. Instead of being painted, cleaned up, and furnished with period pieces, the cabins, sheds, and outbuildings have been made to look as if the original occupants walked out and closed the door, never to return. Cobwebs, dust, and aging relics look as if they have sat undisturbed for decades.

Admission to the museum is free, but donations are greatly appreciated.

Pahranagat National Wildlife Refuge

US Highway 93

Alamo

Directions: Take I-15 north to US 93. Turn left at the exit ramp and take US 93 north toward Alamo. The lake is 60 miles from the turnoff.

Pahranagat National Wildlife Refuge, photo by Kathy Espin

This waterfowl oasis sits smack in the middle of the Mojave Desert. Almost invisible to passersby, the natural wetland is located about 90 miles north of Las Vegas. The 5,380-acre area provides a diverse range of habitats, from desert to cultivated fields, marsh, and open water for a range of wildlife including jackrabbits, bullfrogs, blackbirds, roadrunners, mallards, and hawks. I have even seen migrating blue heron. There are two ponds. The upper lake is the deepest (the last time I went by, however, the lower lake was completely dry). On the south side of the upper lake is a beach area shaded by huge cottonwood trees. It's a popular spot for wading and fishing. Rowboats, canoes, and kayaks are permitted, but no motorized boats. Other spots can be found off the dirt road that runs alongside the upper lake.

Kershaw-Ryan State Park
Caliente
www.parks.nv.gov/kr.htm
775/726-3564
Directions: Take I-15 north to US 93. Turn left at the exit ramp and follow the signs to Caliente. Turn right on NV 317. The park is on the left.

This is a beautiful spot on the north end of Rainbow Canyon, known for its multi-colored sandstone cliffs. Early settlers used the springs located here to feed a pond and grow grape vines, trees, and lawns. The area was homesteaded by the Kershaw family, then sold to the Ryans, who donated the area to the state for a park in 1926. Soon after, the Civilian Conservation Corps developed picnic sites and a small wading pond. In 1935, the state created Kershaw-Ryan State Park and developed a campground, group-use ramada, water system, restrooms, and trails to improve visitor services. Sadly, two bad flash floods in 1984 destroyed nearly all of the facilities. The ramada, water system, and restrooms have been restored and the trails re-established, but the camping facilities still haven't been replaced.

Rachel, Nevada
Area 51
Nevada Highway 375
www.rachel.dreamlandresort.com
Directions: Take I-15 north to US 93. Turn left at the exit ramp and follow the signs toward Caliente and Ely. Turn left at Nevada Highway 375 and follow the signs to Rachel (about 130 miles).

Let's get one thing straight. There is no such thing as Area 51. The official name of the top-secret federal testing facility located at Groom Lake, Nevada, is unknown. It's popularly known as Area 51 because that was the area's designation when it was part of the Nevada Test Site. Today, the unnamed facility is located on the Nellis Air Force Base's bombing and gunnery range.

The area is popular with UFO seekers and government-conspiracy theorists because there have been many reported sightings of unexplained phenomena close by. The extensive security surrounding the testing facility has probably fueled the rumors and legends that have grown up around the place. The strangest experiences I've had in Rachel, the tiny village about 28 miles away, all involved out-of-this-world characters I met at the bar at the Little A'Le Inn. I also got a really spooky feeling once when I realized a man in an unmarked white SUV had been watching my husband and me all night while we camped. I guess we were too near the border of the security buffer zone around the base.

Extraterrestrial Highway (right), courtesy Nevada Commission on Tourism

Little A'Le Inn, Rachel, Nevada (above and right), photos by Kathy Espin

Local landmarks include the notorious black mailbox located about 16 miles from US 93 on Nevada Highway 375 (midway between mileposts 29 and 30). The black mailbox was replaced years ago by a white one by rancher Steve Medlin to whom the box belongs. The area near the mailbox has the best view of the airspace above the testing facility and has been the location of many reported sightings of unexplained phenomena. In an effort to boost tourism, the state renamed Highway 375 "Extraterrestrial Highway" in 1996.

The Little A'Le Inn is a landmark in itself. In the combination bar, coffee shop, motel, and UFO museum, an entire wall is lined with photos that claim to show UFOs. A library of books, articles, magazines, and other printed material is dedicated to all things unexplainable. You can't actually check things out, but they're available for browsing while you eat.

The owners of the Little A'Le Inn, Pat and Joe Travis, play up the UFO connection to the hilt. Outside the establishment is a monument to UFOs erected by 20th Century Fox in 1996 to publicize the movie *Independence Day*. Signs sport pictures of traditional aliens with the saying "Earthlings welcome" and areas of the parking lot are designated for "spaceship parking." Inside are "life-sized" mannequins (who knows how big extraterrestrials really are?) of the small and cuddly version of aliens.

As you may have guessed, I'm not a "believer," but rest assured that many residents and visitors in Rachel are. For a real cultural experience, visit on Labor Day or Memorial Day weekend, when the inn hosts "UFO Friendship" campouts. Some of those people are so far out there that aliens might seem more normal. The Rachel Day celebration on the second Saturday in May is also a must for the curious.

A self-published book by local astronomer and Area 51 authority Chuck Clark, *Area 51 & S-4 Handbook*, is available at the Little A'Le Inn for $15. It mixes hard scientific fact with stories of sightings and wild speculation and is an interesting read. The spiral-bound book also gives detailed directions to the only remaining accessible overlook that gives a view of Groom Lake. The spot at Tikaboo Peak is remote, very difficult to get to, and still more than 25 miles away from the military operation.

Clark's book and other sources can help you find jeep trails that lead to the border of the testing facility's security zone. There you will probably see a white SUV and a guard stationed to watch over the access. You will also see a large sign that says you will be arrested and possibly shot if you proceed farther. Clark assures us the threat is serious.

Beaver Dam State Park

Caliente
775/726-3564
www.parks.nv.gov/bd.htm
Directions: Take I-15 north to US 93. Turn left (north) at the off-ramp and follow the signs to Caliente. After you go through Caliente, watch for the sign on the right that marks the turnoff to Beaver Dam. Follow the gravel road 28 miles to the park entrance.

Beaver Dam, they say, is the most remote and rustic of the Nevada state parks. (Great Basin National Park near Ely is much more remote, I think, but it's a National Park.) At an elevation of 5,000 feet, the 2,393-acre park is forested with pinion and juniper pines and features a lovely stream and reservoir. This is a great spot for photography and nature study and is popular with hikers and campers. Facilities include campgrounds, a group-use area, a day-use picnic area, hiking and educational trails, and hiking access to the reservoir (boats are not recommended because the water is too shallow). Beaver Dam is open year-round, weather permitting, but travel is not advised during winter months. RVs and trailers over 25 feet long are not recommended due to the switchbacks on the narrow gravel road to the park.

Cathedral Gorge State Park

Panaca

775/728-4460

www.parks.nv.gov/cg.htm

Directions: Take I-15 north to US 93. Turn left (north) at the off-ramp and follow the signs to Caliente. After you go through Caliente and Panaca, look for the entrance to the park on the left.

Soft bentonite clay formed into temple-shaped spires by eons of erosion gives this park its name. The scenery is lovely and the campgrounds and picnic areas are shady and cool. Several nice hiking trails wind in and around the formations. The Visitors' Center offers informative displays. Be sure to take some time to explore the maze-like crevices and caverns that erosion has carved into the sides of the gorge. It's a good 10 degrees cooler inside than out. We found a bat cave deep in the wall of the gorge once, where we could sit and watch the bats fly past a hole in the top of the cave. You could see every vein and bone in their wings as they flew through the light.

California—Death Valley

Hotel and motel accommodations are available in Beatty and Tonopah in Nevada. Other accommodations can be found at Furnace Creek in Death Valley, at the Amargosa Opera House and Hotel in Death Valley Junction and at the Longstreet Hotel and Casino on the California/Nevada Border on Nevada Highway 373.

Death Valley National Park

Death Valley
760/786-3200
www.nps.gov/deva
Directions: From Las Vegas, take US 95 north to Highway 267. Turn left at Scotty's Junction.

Only in California would they charge you $10 (per car) to get into a place like Death Valley. The 3.3 million-acre national park is renowned for its desolation and high summer temperatures (averaging around 115 degrees in July). The scenery is incredible: stark, colorful, and haunting. Notable among the numerous hiking trails, scenic drives, and points of interest are Badwater, the lowest point in the western hemisphere; Dante's View, a point 5,000 feet above the valley floor that offers a panorama of the park; and Devil's Golf Course,

Death Valley (above), and Bad Water (right), courtesy Nevada Commission on Tourism

a huge area of rock salt eroded by wind and rain. There are also sand dunes, wooded canyons, and even your occasional spring. Several campgrounds are available, along with two RV parking facilities. There's even a hotel/resort area at Furnace Creek with a real golf course. The usual warnings and precautions about desert travel go double or triple for Death Valley. Always carry water, take care to protect yourself and your children from the sun, stay on the paved roads in the heat of the summer, and if your car breaks down, stay with the vehicle until someone comes along.

Scotty's Castle

Death Valley Ranch
760/786-2395
Hours: Daily, 8 a.m. to 5 p.m.
Directions: Take US 95 north through Beatty to Highway 267 at Scotty's Junction.

Located in Grapevine Canyon, one of the greener and cooler areas of Death Valley (which isn't saying much), Scotty's Castle is a Moorish-style mansion built 75 years ago. Although the castle was built and owned by Albert and Bessie Johnson, their friend, Walter Scott, was designated host to curious visitors who came to watch construction that began in 1927. Scott soon became known as Death Valley Scotty and was so closely connected with the mansion that many people thought he owned it. Opulent materials were shipped in for the project by rail and truck, but construction was interrupted by the financial crash of 1929. The castle was never completed. Now in the hands of the National Park Service, Scotty's Castle is one of the most well-known tourist attractions in Death Valley. Okay, so it's one of the only tourist attractions in Death Valley. Park Rangers dressed in 1930s period costumes conduct regular tours of the mansion, explaining the history and construction. Recently,

Rangers added a "technology tour": a behind-the-scenes look at the basements, tunnels, and utility buildings that focuses on what was considered innovative technology in the 1920s. Due to tricky accessibility, the technology tours are not open to small children and the disabled. Scotty's Castle is open all year round. Services include a gift shop, snack bar, and gas station. A campground is just a few miles away and hotel accommodations are available at Furnace Creek or Stovepipe Wells.

Amargosa Opera House
Death Valley Junction
760/852-4441
www.amargosa-opera-house.com
Hours: Performances at 8:15 p.m. most Saturdays from October through the first two weeks in May.
Directions: Take US 95 north to Nevada Highway 373 (California127). Turn left. Follow this road to Death Valley Junction. Believe me, you can miss it.

Amargosa Opera House, photos by Kathy Espin

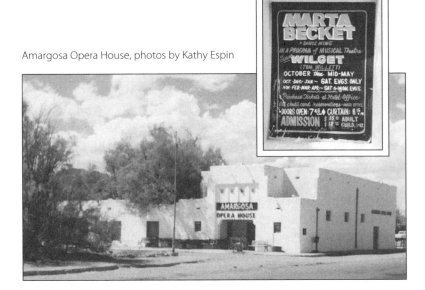

This may be one of the strangest apparitions you'll ever see in the desert. Since 1967, ballerina Marta Becket has performed self-choreographed dance recitals for anyone and everyone (sometimes practically no one) who happened by this remote outpost. She and her MC and comic foil, Thomas Willet, are the entire cast and crew of the theater. After a minor career as a dancer and artist in New York, Becket discovered the abandoned railroad town at Death Valley Junction. At one end of a U-shaped building was an old town hall that Becket made her opera house. The rest of the structure has been converted into an aging hotel. In the theater, spotlights have been fashioned out of old coffee cans and the audience, when there is one, sits on folding chairs. To guard against an empty house, Becket has painted an audience on the walls of the theater. The mural is filled with characters who might have attended an opera during the 16th century, including the king and queen, nobility, bullfighters, monks, and nuns. Inside the double doors she painted a lady dancing to an accompaniment provided by a musician playing an antique musical instrument. Becket is in her 70s now and this one-of-a-kind attraction can't last much longer. Make sure you see it while you still can. Tickets are $15 for adults and $12 for children. The show is not recommended for children under five.

China Ranch and Date Farm

Tecopa
760/852-4415
www.chinaranch.com
Hours: Daily, 9 a.m. to 5 p.m., except Christmas.
Directions: Take I-15 south to Highway 160. Go west (toward Pahrump) to Old Spanish Trail Highway. Take Old Spanish Trail Highway west to Furnace Creek Road; turn left. Follow the signs to China Ranch.

China Ranch and Date Farm (right and below), courtesy China Ranch

Toward the end of the 19th century, a Chinese man left the borax mines in Death Valley and started a farm fed by a tiny spring. After a few years of hard work, he had a thriving enterprise on his hands that was soon stolen by a greedy white man. The ranch was then known as Chinaman's Ranch and has since passed through many hands. This picturesque natural oasis is about 85 miles from Las Vegas on the Nevada/California border. It's now a small family-owned working farm rich with Western history and topography. Huge date palms are skirted with brightly colored petticoats to protect the ripening fruit from the birds. The stream feeds huge cottonwood trees and willows.

Walking and hiking trails take visitors through the date farm and past some spectacular desert vistas and rock formations. A gift shop offers a variety of dates and fresh baked goods, including chocolate chip date cookies and date nut bread. A bed and breakfast inn is also located on the property. This makes a nice stop while exploring Death Valley.

California—Other Areas

Calico Ghost Town

36600 Ghost Town Road
Yermo
800-862-2542
www.calicotown.com
Hours: Daily, 8 a.m. to dusk. Closed Christmas Day.
Directions: Take I-15 south to the Ghost Town Road exit located 10 miles northeast of Barstow, California. Follow the signs.

One-third of the town is the original silver mining town that was founded in 1881. The rest has been carefully reconstructed. Walking tours with Calico's historian examine the life of miners, the famous 20-mule team, and a U.S. Postal mail dog named Dorsey. The Calico Ghost Town Gunfighters create their own version of the shootout at the OK Corral. The Calico-Odessa Railroad operates within the town

Calico Ghost Town, courtesy Calico Ghost Town

limits and offers further details of the site. Maggie's provides a peek inside an underground operation of a hardrock silver mine. Businesses in the town include an 1880s confectionary, a saloon where the sounds of a honky-tonk piano often fill the air, a full-service restaurant, and stores selling leather goods, pottery, basketry, bottles, rocks, and dry goods. South of town is Calico's cemetery. Campgrounds and cabins are available and bunkhouses can accommodate up to 12 people. General admission to Calico is $6 for adults and $3 for children.

Arizona

Grand Canyon

Grand Canyon
www.nps.gov/gcra
928/638-7888
Directions: It's kind of hard to miss. The entrance to the South Rim is 60 miles north of Interstate 40 at Williams via Highway 64, and 80 miles northwest of Flagstaff via Highway 180. The North Rim is 44 miles south of Jacob Lake, Arizona, via Highway 67.

You've seen the photos, so there's no need for me to try to describe the world's grandest of canyons except to say that, when you finally see it in person, you won't believe it. This awe-inspiring canyon is almost a mile deep, 217 miles long, and from four to 18 miles wide.

It was carved over centuries by the Colorado River that now flows along the canyon floor. Tour operators take folks white-water rafting along the river way below. Other guided tours take you from the rim to the Hualapai Indian reservation deep in the canyon. You can get there by car, plane, bus, or helicopter (see Tours in Appendix II, beginning on pg. 181).

Two areas serve most of the visitors to the canyon. The

South Rim is the most popular and populated. Just outside the gates is Grand Canyon Village, an entire town developed just to serve tourists. Hotels, motels, and restaurants abound. Inside the park, on the edge of the canyon, is a lodge and museum. The South Rim is open 24 hours a day, 365 days a year. Services are available and facilities are open year round, even though snow sometimes makes access difficult.

The North Rim is not as crowded but it's harder to reach. Also, the elevation on the North Rim is at 8,000 feet so snow

Grand Canyon, photos courtesy Grand Canyon National Park

closes that side much of the year. The visitor facilities are only open from mid-May to mid-October. Weather permitting, the North Rim is open only for day use after mid-October and no services or overnight facilities are available inside the park. The road from Jacob Lake to the North Rim (Highway 67) is subject to closure with little or no notice in the winter.

Hiking, camping, and just gawking at the view are popular pastimes in the park. On the South Rim, a free shuttle service is available year round that goes out to Grand Canyon Village and in to the South Kaibab Trailhead and seasonally to other spots. No shuttle buses serve the North Rim.

Chloride Mining Town

Chloride
928/565-2204
www.chloridearizona.com
Directions: Take US 93 across Hoover Dam to the Chloride turnoff, three-fourths of a mile past mile marker 52. Turn left onto Chloride Road (County Road 125). Travel about four miles to Chloride.

Chloride is a much more charming town than its name would indicate. The town was named for the ore in which miners found silver, gold, lead, zinc, and turquoise from the mid-1800s. The town started with a silver strike in the 1860s and continued to grow until the mines shut down in the mid-1940s. When most of the residents left for jobs in other towns, it looked like Chloride would become a ghost town, but retirees, artists, and others found the weather, scenery, and remote location attractive and the population began to climb again. Today, a year-round population of about 150 swells to 250 in the winter months when the snowbirds arrive from up north.

In the 1960s, artist Roy Purcell led a band of hippies who settled for a while in Chloride. During their stay, Purcell painted murals on the rocks high above the town. The "Chloride Murals" can still be seen but aren't easy to reach. Ancient petroglyphs are also located in this area.

Today, the town's primary industry is tourism with restaurants, bars, gift shops, and restored buildings such as the train station, bank, and post office. The requisite gunfights are staged regularly. Shop owners sell handmade jewelry, antiques, and just plain junk. There are two restaurants, two bars, several gift shops, a convenience store, a fire station, and a few interesting tourist sights, including the historic post office and train station.

Trails are open for hiking, biking, off-road riding, and horseback riding. Nearby are two BLM campgrounds: Windy Point and Packsaddle. From these sites you can see land in four states: Arizona, California, Nevada, and Utah.

Oatman, Arizona

928/768-6222

www.oatmangoldroad.com

Directions: Take US 93 south and turn left on Nevada Highway 163. Take the highway through Laughlin, Nevada, and across the bridge. Turn right (south) on US Highway 95, then left on Oatman Road. Follow the signs to Oatman.

Oatman is a popular setting for TV and movie Westerns thanks to its well-preserved old buildings. The town was once a thriving gold-mining town and the descendants of prospectors' burros now wander the streets to the delight of visitors. The town is named for the Oatman family, who never actually lived there. Six members of the family died in an Indian massacre near Gila Bend, Arizona. The residents named the town to honor the fallen. The Oatman Hotel, the oldest two-story adobe building in Mojave County, was built in 1902 and named the Durlin Hotel. Clark Gable and Carole Lombard spent their wedding night in the hotel after being married in Kingman, Arizona, on March 29, 1939; the marriage came to an end in 1942 when Lombard died in an airplane crash in the Spring Mountains west of Las Vegas. The hotel is supposed to be haunted, not by either of the Gables, but by an old miner who drank himself to death there. Here, authentic old buildings have been turned into shops, bars, and restaurants. See more gunfighter showdowns in a day than ever actually occurred in the history of the West.

Utah

Snow Canyon State Park

Santa Clara

435/628-2255

www.stateparks.utah.gov

Directions: Take I-15 north to St. George, Utah. Turn left on Utah Highway 18 (Bluff Street). Turn left on Utah Highway 416. Snow Canyon is 11 miles northwest of St. George.

Want to get away from the crowds? This is the place. Snow Canyon isn't easy to find, which might be why it's rarely crowded. Here, red and white Navajo sandstone creates some incredible scenery. To one side of the canyon are the Red Mountains and a few miles away are the White Hills. Eroded sandstone rocks of both colors make up the cliffs on either side of the valley, contrasted against the

Red sand dunes in Snow Canyon State Park (facing page), and Snow Canyon State Park trail (right), courtesy Utah Department of Parks and Recreation

mass of black lava from a cluster of volcanoes beyond. The lava, plus cinder cones and lava caves, are the main points of interest. Many kids like the red sand dunes the best. This quiet little park offers a campground, restrooms with flush toilets, hot showers, and RV spaces.

Zion Canyon National Park

Springdale
435/772-3256
www.nps.gov/zion
Directions: Take I-15 north past St. George, Utah (about 120 miles). Take exit 40 at Utah Highway 9, about 40 miles east of town.

Within Zion National Park's 229 square miles is a spectacular cliff-and-canyon landscape and wilderness full of the unexpected, such as the world's largest arch, Kolob Arch, with a span of 310 feet, along with waterfalls and hanging gardens. Mule deer, golden eagles, and mountain lions inhabit the park. Mukuntuweap National Monument was proclaimed on July 31,

1909, and was incorporated into Zion National Monument on March 18, 1918. The area was designated a national park on November 19, 1919.

Hikes led by park rangers are specially designed to be fun and educational. Inquire at the visitor's center near the I-15 entrance. Activities beyond the usual include rock climbing, river tubing, and swimming. Zion is a great place for rock hunting and photography.

Near the entrance to the park, the Zion Canyon Giant Screen Theater shows adventure films on a Cinemax screen. One film features a virtual tour of the park. For information call 435/772-2400.

Tuacahn Amphitheater
Ivins
800-746-9882
www.tuacahn.org
Directions: Take I-15 north to St. George, Utah (about 120 miles). Take Utah Highway 18 north out of St. George (Bluff Street). Turn left off Utah Highway18 toward Ivins. Follow the signs to Tuacahn.

At Tuacahn is a 2,000-seat outdoor amphitheater set in a beautiful red sandstone box canyon. The facility opened in 1995 with the production "Utah!" that told the story of the settlement of Utah by the founders of the Mormon Church. The classic tale of hardship and triumph was told in music with the help of pyrotechnics, live animals, a huge cast, and the re-creation of a flash flood with 60,000 gallons of water pouring across the stage. The show was a hit for many years, and the company has since expanded to offer other family-friendly productions such as "The King and I," "The Wizard of Oz," and "The Unsinkable Molly Brown." The season runs from June to August. Tickets start at $25 for adults and $15 for children under 12. Tickets for children sitting on a parent's lap run from $5 to $10.

Bryce Canyon National Park
Visitors' Center
435/834-5322
www.nps.gov/brca/
Directions: Take I-15 north through St. George, Utah. Turn right on Utah Highway 9 at Hurricane. Turn left on US 89 at Mt. Carmel Junction, then right (east) on Utah Highway 12. Follow the signs to Bryce Canyon. The canyon is 270 miles from Las Vegas.

Winter and summer, Bryce Canyon is a beautiful place to enjoy the great outdoors. The park is named for one of a series of horseshoe-shaped amphitheaters carved from the eastern edge of the Paunsaugunt Plateau. Erosion has shaped limestone, sandstone, and mudstone into thousands of spires, fins, pinnacles, and mazes. Collectively called "hoodoos," these unique formations come in a range of colors from white to bright red. Camping facilities, hotels, motels, and RV camps are available, as well as an array of services and rentals for biking, snowmobiling, and river rafting. The Bryce Canyon historic lodge is open April 1 through October 31 with 114 rooms, including suites and rustic cabins.

When Price Is No Object

People with lots of money find Las Vegas a great place to shed some of it and the local tourism industry is happy to help out. People we fondly call "high rollers" can find the best services in the world at their beck and call if they are willing to pay the price—and they often are. Deluxe family services are included. Here are some options for people who really want to live it up with their kids. Don't we all?

Grand Canyon Helicopter Tours

Sundance Helicopters
800-659-1881
www.helicoptour.com

Sundance Helicopters is one of many services offering tours of the Grand Canyon. The company's VIP Deluxe Champagne Tour is perfect for the family that likes to keep the great outdoors at a distance.

For $379 per person, a limo picks you up at your hotel for a ride to the helicopter pad. There, you get a quick safety lesson before you're strapped into the six-seat Eurocopter Astar that lifts off and skims over the city toward Lake Mead. The 45-minute flight takes in Lake Mead and a fly-by of Hoover Dam. Soon, the pilot points out the wall of mountains that forms the western edge of the canyon. While Wagner's "Ride of the Valkyries" plays over headsets, the helicopter climbs to clear the

Grand Canyon Helicopter tour, photos courtesy Sundance Helicopters

ridge, then drops back down for a breathtaking in-your-face first glimpse of the Grand Canyon. After a quick fly-over, including some up-close time with the canyon walls, the pilot makes the 3,200-foot descent into the canyon.

The landing site is on the bank of the Colorado River. The short but steep trail from the landing pad to the boat dock on the water is the only time passengers' shoes touch Mother Earth during the entire trip. From the dock, a pontoon boat takes passengers on a river tour complete with non-alcoholic champagne and picnic lunches. After the 30-minute boat ride, it's back to the dock for the flight back to Las Vegas.

Sundance and other companies also offer flights over the Las Vegas Strip and other local sights (see Tours in Appendix II, beginning on pg. 181).

Camp Hyatt

Hyatt Regency Hotel
Lake Las Vegas Resort
800-554-9288
www.lakelasvegas.hyatt.com

The Hyatt Regency, a Mobil four-star resort, sits on a 320-acre man-made lake just west of Lake Mead. Across the lake from the hotel is an exclusive residential area where Celine Dion recently moved in. The hotel offers a full-service childcare program called Camp Hyatt, which offers supervised activities

Camp Hyatt, courtesy Hyatt Regency Lake Las Vegas

every kid would enjoy. The program is tailored to the wishes of the children. Some of the activities include field trips, swimming and water-slide fun, board games, sand- and mud-castle building, field games, and karaoke contests. During good weather, field trips include frog and lizard hunts. When the weather is bad (in our area that means "too hot"), the hotel's ballroom is used for kickball and other active games. The camp is open to children three (potty trained) to 12 and in itself is not all that expensive. The cost is $27 per child for three hours or $40 for four hours. The catch is that the children have to be hotel guests. Rooms at the Hyatt can run more than $500 per night.

VIP Balloon Ride

D&R Balloons
702/248-7609
www.lasvegasballoonrides.com

Several companies offer one-hour hot-air balloon rides to the lake or surrounding mountains for about $150 per person, but D&R has come up with a special package for the family with more money than time. The package was designed for couples, but can be negotiated for families. For $1,500 for two people, D&R will pick you up in a limo, serve Dom Perignon during the ride (not for the kids, of course) and provide upscale gifts. At the airfield, a red carpet leads to the balloon that is ready to go. More snacks are served on the way back to the hotel. For the regular flight, you have to wait around for the balloon to inflate (you can help if you like) and champagne is served in a traditional ceremony at the end of the flight that takes more time. With the VIP flight, you're back in the casino in an hour or two. The regular trip takes three hours or more.

Ground school, courtesy Richard Petty Driving Experience

Richard Petty Driving Experience

6975 Speedway Boulevard
800-237-3889
www.1800bepetty.com
Hours: By appointment.
Directions: Take I-15 north to the Las Vegas Speedway turn-off.

Children 16 and older with a valid driver's license can have the thrill of driving a real NASCAR racecar at the Richard Petty Driving Experience. The Rookie Experience starts at $349 and includes all the equipment. Prices go all the way up to $2,999 for the Advanced Racing Experience, a two-day training program for serious racers. Each program starts with ground school before quickly putting participants behind the wheel. The more you pay, the more time you get behind the wheel. Ride-alongs are available for children 14 and older.

Driving 101

6915 Speedway Boulevard
877-374-8310
www.driving101.com
Directions: Take I-15 north to the Las Vegas Speedway turn-off.

The ultimate adrenaline rush at Driving 101 will cost you between $375 for Racing 101 to $8,999 for the two-day Extreme Racing Experience. The program is quite similar to the one at the Richard Petty School, except that the cars used are the faster Indy-style. Ride-alongs start at $75 and go up to $179. For the ride-alongs, children must be at least five feet tall and weigh at least 100 pounds.

Sandy Valley Ranch

1411 Kingston Road
Sandy Valley, Nevada
702/631-0463
877-726-3998
www.sandyvalleyranch.com
Hours: Vary. Mostly by appointment.
Directions: Take I-15 south to Nevada Highway 161 (Exit 12); turn right. Turn left on Kingston Road.

Sandy Valley represents the outback parts of Nevada that tourists rarely see. It's large, flat, and, well, sandy. The ranch is a working dude ranch where you can join in on cattle roundups, trail rides, and wagon rides. A Sunset Dinner Trail Ride includes a horseback ride or wagon ride, plus barbecue and singing and cowboy poetry around a campfire. The sunset dinners are $138 per person and participating in a cattle roundup runs from $500 for a one-person exclusive to $350 per day per person for nine to 12 people. A riding lesson and one-hour trail ride runs $45. The

Sandy Valley Ranch, courtesy Sandy Valley Ranch

ranch also offers a bed and breakfast option that starts at $160 per night for two. There's quite a list of add-ons. Want a cowboy to play the guitar during dinner? $200. A massage before bed? $100. Limo to and from the ranch? $445. There is a petting zoo for children but only children 11 and older can participate in the horseback adventures.

Grand Canyon Ultimate Helicopter Tour and Cowboy Ranch Adventure
888-609-5665
www.all-las-vegas-tours.com

This is the ultimate City Slicker experience. A helicopter picks you up in Las Vegas and flies you over the Grand Canyon, then touches down at a dude ranch nearby. Accommodations at the ranch are air-conditioned luxury cabins with fireplaces. Ranch staff provides tours via horse-drawn wagon and optional horseback rides are available for an additional fee. A barbecue steak dinner is served and cowboys entertain by the campfire at night. A hearty ranch breakfast the next morning precedes the flight back to Las Vegas. Prices vary seasonally, but start at $375 for adults and $314 for children under 14. Lap children are free, but why you'd take a baby on a trip like this, I don't know.

Bar 10 Ranch
Grand Canyon, Arizona
800-582-4139
www.bar10.com

The Bar 10 Ranch is a working cattle ranch nine miles from the north rim of the Grand Canyon. It's a 50-minute flight from Las Vegas (there's a landing strip for private planes) or a two-hour drive from St. George, Utah, over 80 miles of dirt road. The ranch is fully self-sustained with its own power and water source. Roping and riding lessons are offered. River rafting tours of the Colorado River and helicopter tours of the Grand Canyon are available. Overnight package includes accommodations, three meals, horseback riding, ranch activities, hiking, skeet shooting, horseshoes, billiards, volleyball, and a country-western evening program with singing, clogging, trick roping, and good ole Western humor for $139.95 per person. Three- and four-day river rafting trips run from $790 per person and up. Dinner, lodging, and breakfast starts at $84.95 per person. These prices do not include transportation to the ranch. Ranch visits are not recommended for children under eight.

Calendar of Events

January

Chinese New Year

4205 Spring Mountain Road
Las Vegas
702/221-8448

The Asian-Pacific Cultural Center is the host to this annual festival. The Chinese New Year does not have the same date as the Western New Year and changes from year to year. The festival features exhibits, dances, Asian food, and Mahjong tournaments.

Martin Luther King Day Parade

Downtown
Las Vegas
www.kingweeklasvegas.com

Held annually on Martin Luther King Day, the parade begins at 9:30 a.m. on Hoover Avenue and Fourth Street in downtown Las Vegas.

February

Las Vegas Marathon
702/876-3870

The 26.2-mile marathon begins in the nearby town of Sloan. The two-day marathon and festival has stands for spectators set up on portions of the Las Vegas Strip.

March

NASCAR Weekend
Las Vegas Motor Speedway
Las Vegas
702/644-4444

The NASCAR Nextel Cup and Busch Grand National races are held annually at the beginning of March.

St. Patrick's Day Parade
Downtown
Las Vegas
702/678-5600

A parade and festival held on the Saturday before St. Patrick's Day. The parade runs along Fremont Street in downtown Las Vegas.

April

Mardi Gras Comes to Vegas
Fremont Street Experience
Downtown
Las Vegas
702/678-5742

Parade and festival held annually during Mardi Gras season.

Clark County Fair
Clark County Fairgrounds
1301 West Whipple Avenue
Logandale, Nevada
888-876-3247
www.ccfair.com

The Clark County Fair is held annually in mid-April.

May

Cinco de Mayo
Freedom Park
Mojave Road and Washington Avenue
Las Vegas
702/649-8553

This annual festival is held each year on the closest Sunday to May 5 and features marching bands, carnival games, exhibits, and ethnic foods.

Jazz in the Park

Clark County Government Center
500 South Grand Central Parkway
Las Vegas
702/455-8242

Local and international jazz artists perform Saturday evenings from mid-May to mid-June. Admission is free.

Rachel Day Celebration

Rachel, Nevada
775/729-2515
www.rachel.dreamlandresort.com

Held the second Saturday in May, the annual celebration features a parade, games, sales, raffles, and live music. For information call the Little A'Le Inn at the number above.

Creole Festival Internationale

Sunset Park
2601 Sunset Road
702/455-8161
www.starfactreefoundation.org

Food, vendors, New Orleans-style music celebrating Creole culture. Featuring an art exhibition, Louisiana games, face-painting, and mask-making for children.

Southern Nevada Cultural History Fair

Springs Preserve
3701 West Alta Drive
702/822-8312

Food, arts and crafts, entertainment, culture, and education. Dozens of museums and cultural performance groups; scholars discuss the history of Las Vegas.

June

Fishing Derby for Children

Sunset Park Lake
Sunset Road and Eastern Avenue
Las Vegas
702/455-8289

A free competition held on the second Saturday in June at 6:30 a.m. hosts 1,500 children as contestants.

July

Red, White, and Boom

Desert Breeze Park
8425 Spring Mountain Road
Las Vegas
702/455-8206

This is one of the best and largest Fourth of July celebrations in Las Vegas. This festival features fireworks, kids' games and rides, food, a car show, live music, and more.

Fourth of July Parade
Summerlin
Hillspoint Road
Las Vegas
702/341-5500
www.summerlin.com

Traditional patriotic parade with a small-town feel.

World Figure-Skating Champions Tour
Thomas & Mack Center
Las Vegas
702/895-3900

Top ice skaters perform annually at the Thomas & Mack Center.

August

Kidzmania
Cashman Field Center
850 Las Vegas Boulevard North
Las Vegas
702/233-8338

A two-day event with activities for both children and parents. Kids can participate in a petting zoo, essay contest, and more. Parents can participate in seminar-style presentations on a variety of parenting issues.

September

Summerlin's All-You-Can-Eat Ice Cream Festival
Summerlin Centre Community Park
Las Vegas
702/933-7777

The annual festival features all-you-can-eat ice cream cones, sundaes and floats. There're ice-cream eating contests and performances by the Nevada Ballet Theatre.

Miss Kitty's Jeans to Jewels
Bitter Root Ranch
Las Vegas
702/259-3741

Features country dancing, music, and food. For information call the number above.

Mexican Independence Day
Freedom Park
Mojave Road and Washington Avenue
Las Vegas
702/649-8553

The annual festival is held on September 16 and celebrates the independence of Mexico. The festival features music, authentic foods, entertainment, and exhibits.

The Greek Food Festival
St. John's Greek Orthodox Church
5300 South El Camino Road
Las Vegas
702/221-8245

A special celebration of Greek cuisine is held annually in mid-September.

San Gennaro Feast
Las Vegas
702/286-4944
www.sangennarofeast.net

An annual festival in honor of Saint Gennaro features Italian cuisine, live national acts, and a carnival. The location varies.

Utah Shakespearean Festival
351 West Cedar Street
Cedar City, Utah
800-PLAYTIX (752-9849)
www.bard.org

Featuring live Shakespearean and modern classic theatre, the festival offers meet-and-greets with the actors, a Royal Feaste, and backstage tours.

October

Las Vegas Invitational
Las Vegas
702/242-3000
lvfounders@lvfcgolf.com

Top PGA Tour Golf Professionals compete for a top prize of $720,000 and a total purse of $4 million.

Age of Chivalry—Renaissance Festival
Sunset Park
Sunset Road and Eastern Avenue
Las Vegas
702/455-4200
www.lvrenfair.com

Sunset Park becomes a Renaissance Village with artisans, craftsmen, magicians, comedians, and jousting tournaments. This event is held annually in mid-October.

Art in the Park
Bicentennial Park
Utah and Colorado Streets
Boulder City, Nevada
702/332-8245

This annual festival features arts, crafts, and food.

Las Vegas Century Bicycle Ride

Las Vegas
702/252-4663
sarahrmh@cox.net

Participants can choose from five distances ranging from 22 to 108 miles.

Las Vegas Comedy Festival

Stardust Hotel and Casino
Las Vegas
702/736-6595
mary@laughacrossamerica.com

Amateur and professional comedians compete and take part in 12 comedy showcases, 16 seminars, and a banquet. Use parental discretion. This festival is not recommended for young children.

Halloween Creature Feature

Freedom Park
Mojave Road and Washington Avenue
Las Vegas
702/229-6729

On the two Saturdays before Halloween, Freedom Park hosts this event featuring ghosts, goblins, and storytellers. Children wearing costumes are considered for prizes.

Sunny 106.5 Safe Street

Opportunity Village
6300 West Oakey Boulevard
Las Vegas
702/259-3700
www.opportunityvillage.org

Safe alternative for trick-or-treaters 12 and under.

Lobster Fair

Christ Episcopal Church
2000 South Maryland Parkway
702/735-7655

Lobsters, sourdough bread, craft items, and entertainment throughout the day.

Summerlin Art Festival

Summerlin Centre Community Park
1800 Town Center Drive (between Charleston Boulevard and Sahara Avenue)
702/791-4437

Outdoor festival of art, music, entertainment, and food. Original art by more than 100 artists from around the country. Live performances by the Academy of Nevada Ballet Theatre.

November

Ethel M® Chocolates Light the Night Holiday Spectacular

2 Cactus Garden Drive
Henderson
702/435-2655
tmaruca@kirvindoak.com

The lighting of the Ethel M® Chocolates Botanical Cactus Garden features holiday lights, music, Santa, and chocolates. The garden is lit from sundown until 10 p.m. and runs from mid-November through the first week of January.

Holiday Feast

Nevada School of the Arts
315 South 7th Street
Las Vegas
702/386-2787
nsa@wizard.com

This gala holiday feast features talents of students at the Nevada School of the Arts.

Western Heritage Festival

Community College of Southern Nevada
3200 East Cheyenne Avenue
North Las Vegas

The Community College of Southern Nevada hosts this festival featuring arts, crafts, poetry reading, and music. The hot-air balloons mark the arrival of the festival.

Magical Forest

Opportunity Village
6300 West Oakey Avenue
Las Vegas
702/255-8733
www.opportunityvillage.org

Each year from the end of November to the end of December, Opportunity Village turns into a Christmas Wonderland with a carousel, train rides, and more.

December

GVHS Winter Dance Concert

460 Arroyo Grande Boulevard
Henderson
702/799-0950
suzraymond@yahoo.com

The students at Green Valley High School have a chance to show their talents as dancers and choreographers at this dance concert.

Las Vegas Philharmonic

Holiday Celebration Concerts
Las Vegas
702/895-2787
www.LVPhil.com

This holiday celebration concert has become a community tradition. Seating is reserved.

Christmas Train Show

Henderson Convention Center
200 Water Street
702/566-0856
wescvegas@cox.net

Model trains of all scales are on display. The event includes a train swap meet and arts and crafts vendors.

Children's Christmas Parade

Water Street
Henderson
702/565-8951
www.hendersonchamber.com

Sponsored by the Henderson Chamber of Commerce, the parade starts at noon on a Saturday in mid-December.

Shows and Tours

Shows

Most Las Vegas stage productions are not suitable for children, but a few make for delightful family entertainment. The following shows are not only G-rated, but also have content children will enjoy.

Lance Burton: Master Magician
Monte Carlo Hotel & Casino
702/730-7160

Big-stage magic show with lots of charm and family appeal.

The Mac King Comedy Magic Show
Harrah's Las Vegas
702/369-5111

One-man afternoon comedy/magic show that will steal your heart. Best entertainment bargain in town.

Blue Man Group
Luxor Hotel & Casino
702/262-4400

Off-beat, original, and creatively funny.
Low-tech effects are as stunning as the high-
tech ones.

Mystère
Treasure Island Resort & Casino (TI)
702/392-1999

This riveting animal-free European-style
circus has been seen around the world.

Tournament of Kings
Excalibur Hotel & Casino
702/597-7600

Knights of the Round Table joust and
sword fight while the audience feasts medieval style (no utensils).

Ronn Lucas
Rio All-Suite Hotel & Casino
702/777-7776

A little racy but fine for any child old enough for "The Simp-
sons." Ventriloquist and his pals pack in the punch lines.

Tours

Adventure Las Vegas

702/869-9991
888-846-4747
www.adventurelasvegas.com

ATV, raft, kayak, mountain bike, hike, or ride horseback at Red Rock Canyon, Grand Canyon.

Adventure Photo Tours, Inc.

702/889-8687
www.adventurephototours.com

Half-day and full-day tours to Red Rock Canyon National Conservation Area, Joshua Tree Forest in the Spring Mountains, and the Goodsprings Valley ghost mines. Full-day tours are offered to Grand Canyon, Valley of Fire, the Eldorado Canyon abandoned mines, Logan Wash, and more.

All Las Vegas Tours

702/233-1627
www.all-las-vegas-tours.com

Half- or full-day adventure and sightseeing trips, tours, and activities in and around Las Vegas, the Grand Canyon, Hoover Dam, and Death Valley. White-water rafting trips; off-road Humvee tours; glider, airplane, and helicopter flights; personalized nature tours, sky diving, horseback riding, karting, and lake cruises.

American Adventure Tours, Inc.

702/876-4600

www.americanadventuretours.com

A variety of tours including the Grand Canyon; the Colorado River; Moab, Utah; Lake Mead; and Lake Powell. Tours range from half-day to 14-day excursions: ATV, Jeep, mountain bike, horseback riding, hiking, backpacking, watercraft, snowmobile, white-water rafting, float trips, and a thrill-ride tour that includes roller coasters, bungy jumping, sling-shot, and more.

American Alpine Institute

800-424-2249

www.mtnguide.com

Rock climbing instruction at Red Rock Canyon.

American Angler Guide Service

702/630-2237

www.americanangler.net

Guided fishing trips on Lake Mead for stripers and large-mouth bass. All necessary bait and tackle are provided, as well as fileting and packing of each customer's catch.

Ancient Wisdom Tours

435/544-3311

800-871-6811

Also known as Utah Trail Resorts in Kanab, Utah, offers survival-skills instruction and wilderness adventure tours.

Angler's Edge Guide Service

702/285-2814

www.fish-anglersedge.com

Guided fishing trips for stripers and largemouth bass on Lake Mead and Lake Mohave. All necessary equipment provided.

Annie Bananie's Wild West Tours

702/804-9755

www.anniebananie.com

A 6½-hour bus tour of Lake Mead National Recreation Area and Valley of Fire. Includes lunch, hotel pickup, a guide, and a stop at a natural desert oasis.

Anywhere Tours of Las Vegas

702/566-7834

866-269-8687

www.anywheretours.com

ATV Action Tours, Inc.

702/566-7400

888-288-5200

www.atvactiontours.com

Offers a variety of scenic land tours via off-road vehicles, white-water river rafting and Sea-Doo personal watercraft adventures.

Best Las Vegas Tours

702/567-8259
866-688-BEST (2378)
www.bestlasvegastours.com

Grand Canyon, Hoover Dam and Las Vegas sightseeing tours.

Black Canyon/Willow Beach River Adventures

702/294-1414
www.blackcanyonadventures.com

Smooth-water float trip from Hoover Dam to Willow Beach Marina on the Colorado River, south of Hoover Dam.

Blindfold Tours & Guide Service, Inc.

866-804-1625
www.blindfoldtours.com

Guided four-wheel-drive tours around the Kanab, Utah, area, Bryce Canyon National Park, Zion National Park, the Grand Canyon, and the Grand Staircase-Escalante National Monument. Trips range from 1½ hours to all-day tours of scenic vistas, slot canyons, dinosaur tracks, and American Indian rock art. Trips are available for all ages and abilities. Weekend getaway packages are also available.

Colorado River Tours

702/291-0026
www.coloradorivertour.com

Gold mine tours in historic Eldorado Canyon. Visitors may

also canoe or kayak at the Blue Water Coves of the Colorado River at the base of the Grand Canyon. Shuttles and guides are available.

Cowboy Trail Rides

702/387-2457
www.redrockranch.org

Scenic horseback rides daily at Red Rock Canyon and Kyle Canyon Road on the way to Mount Charleston. A Red Rock sunset dinner ride Tuesday through Saturday evenings features a two-hour rim ride topped with a Western-style barbecue. Wagon rides, seasonal sleigh rides, and weddings are also available.

Desert Fox Tours

702/361-0676
www.vegashummertours.com

Offers three-hour off-road Humvee tours through Red Rock Canyon; search for wild mustangs along the way.

Double Decker Bus Tours

702/384-3325
877-502-8900
www.comedyondeck.com

VIP double decker bus tours of Hoover Dam and Las Vegas featuring comedians as guides.

Drive-Yourself Tours, Inc.
702/565-8761
www.drive-yourselftours.com

Offers nine different audiotapes with maps for self-guided tours around Las Vegas and the Grand Canyon. Cassette tapes are $14.95 each.

First Travel Tours
702/228-9902
800-255-7101
www.firsttraveltours.com

Journey to the Grand Canyon in a helicopter via Hoover Dam, Rainbow Canyon, and Lake Mead to the West Rim, then down into the Grand Canyon. Then fly to a 105,000-acre ranch for a barbecue lunch. Add on an ATV- or horseback-guided tour.

A Grand Canyon Tour 4u
702/233-1627
800-566-5868
www.atour4u.com

Tours of Grand Canyon, Death Valley, Hoover Dam, and more. Horseback and Hummer tours plus Colorado River rafting.

Grand Canyon Tour Company
702/655-6060
800-222-6966
www.grandcanyontourcompany.com

Daily tours by airplane, bus, and helicopter to the South Rim, Grand Canyon West, Hoover Dam, and Laughlin.

Grand Canyon Tour Guide
866-868-7786
www.grand-canyon-tour-guide.com

Guided sightseeing tours to Grand Canyon from Las Vegas.

#1 Grand Canyon Tours
702/233-1627
888-TOURSTORE (868-7786)
www.1-grand-canyon-tours.com

Grand Canyon tours from Las Vegas. Ask about 2-for-1 deals.

Hike This!
702/393-4453
www.hikethislasvegas.com

Single-day guided hiking tours in Red Rock Canyon for fitness and exercise.

Hoover Dam Tour Company
702/361-7628
888-512-0075
www.hooverdamtourcompany.com

Daily tours to Hoover Dam, Grand Canyon, and Lake Mead by motorcoach, airplane, or helicopter.

Jackson Hole Mountain Guides and Climbing School
800-239-7642
www.jhmg.com

One-day guided hikes or scrambles; one-day guided technical climbs; and basic, intermediate, and advanced climbing courses in Red Rock Canyon.

#1 Las Vegas Tours
702/233-1627
800-566-5868
www.1-las-vegas-shows.com

A selection of adventure and sightseeing tours from Las Vegas to the Grand Canyon, Hoover Dam, Lake Mead, Death Valley, Red Rock Canyon, Eldorado Canyon, and Joshua Tree forests. Try personal watercrafts, white-water rafting, horseback riding, helicopter and plane flights, bus and off-road Jeep tours, all-terrain vehicles, kayaking, and lake cruises.

Nevada Tours
888-222-2858
www.wildnvegas.net

Grand Canyon, Hoover Dam, Lake Mead, and Las Vegas city tours.

Outdoor Source Flyfishers
702/499-8921
www.outdoorsource.net

A guided fly-fishing service in the Las Vegas and southern

Utah area. Fly-fishing lessons are available for novices. Group, family, and club picnics and company retreats are also offered.

Paradise Found Tours

702/363-1407
888-607-9374
www.paradisefoundtours.com

See Hoover Dam, Grand Canyon and Las Vegas sights.

Pink Jeep Tours Las Vegas, Inc.

702/895-6777
888-900-4480
www.pinkjeep.com

Professionally guided sightseeing tours of Red Rock Canyon, the Valley of Fire, the Grand Canyon, and other sites in custom Jeeps and sport utility vehicles.

Rebel Adventure Tours

702/380-6969
www.rebeladventuretours.com

Jet Skis, white-water rafting, mountain biking, helicopters, sailplanes, gold mining, ATVs, customized Hummers, and horseback riding.

Rocky Trails

702/869-9991
888-86-ROCKY (76259)
www.rockytrails.com

Western ranch experiences, horseback and wagon rides, and BBQ parties.

Sagebrush Ranch Trail Rides
702/645-9422

A variety of trail rides including a mountain-range breakfast ride and sunset steak-dinner ride. Children and novice riders are welcome. Lessons and daily rides are available. Call Jacque at the number above.

Showtime Tours
702/895-9976
www.showtimetourslasvegas.com

Sightseeing experiences ranging from half-day to full-day tours featuring Hoover Dam, Lake Mead, the Grand Canyon, river raft floats, Laughlin, ghost mines/ATV excursions, and day and night city tours of Las Vegas.

Silver State "Old West" Tours
702/798-7788
www.silverstatetours.com

Located in Spring Mountain Ranch State Park, scenic horseback trail rides go to Red Rock Canyon. Trail, stagecoach, and wagon rides; Western barbecue events; and roping contests seven days a week.

Treasure Tours of Nevada
702/360-7978
www.lasvegasinfos.com

Tour operator in English and German language. Hotel and show ticket service.

UnoMundo
702/496-8309
www.unomundo.net

Leisurely tours of the Southwest for photographers.

Vegastours.com
702/719-6837
866-218-6877
www.vegastours.com

Offering discount tours to Grand Canyon by airplane, helicopter, or bus.

Walking Tours
702/875-4141
www.parks.nv.gov/smr.htm

These quarter-mile 45-minute tours at Spring Mountain Ranch State Park lead to the 1860s blacksmith's shop, the second-oldest building in the Las Vegas Valley, and Lake Harriet. Tours are offered daily: Monday through Friday at noon, 1 p.m., and 2 p.m., and Saturday and Sunday at noon, 1 p.m., 2 p.m., and 3 p.m.

Child Care

The following facilities are licensed and bonded by Clark County. Some claim that their staff has security clearance through the Sheriff's Department and the FBI. Always ask for documentation to verify the current status of the licenses and Sheriff and FBI checks.

These referral listings DO NOT constitute an endorsement of the facilities listed. All facilities must meet minimum standards established for the protection of the children receiving care. Parents are encouraged to make personal visits before selecting a facility for their child.

Cinderella Careskool
702/732-0230

Drop-ins welcome anytime with no registration fee. Open 24 hours. Accepts kids two to 12 years old.

Dial a Granny
702/376-5229

Service to homes or hotels. Licensed and bonded since 1980. Open 24 hours, seven days per week.

Grandma Thompson's Romp 'n' Play
702/735-0176

Offers a "home-away-from-home" atmosphere. One block from the Strip. Open 24 hours.

Affectionate Hotel & Home Childcare
702/838-1268

Babysitters come to your hotel and are licensed and cleared by the FBI. Staffmembers have completed Sheriff background checks, hold health cards, and are trained in CPR. Open 24 hours.

Around the Clock Child Care
702/365-1040

In business for more than ten years and available 24 hours. Cleared through the Sheriff's office and FBI, licensed, and bonded.

Competent, Compassionate Care Givers
702/699-9924

Licensed and bonded, first-aid- and CPR-certified babysitting. Available 24 hours. Foreign languages on request.

MGM Grand Youth Center
702/891-7777

For children from three to 12 years old, featuring Super Nintendo, foosball, air hockey, pool table, floor hockey, basketball, dodge-ball, two-story playhouse, puzzles, dollhouse, dinosaurs, puppets, blocks, and much more. Available to registered guests of MGM Grand and, on a limited basis, guests of other hotels. Current rate is $7 per hour for hotel guests, $9 per hour for non-guests. Maximum of five hours.

Gold Coast Hotel
702/367-7111

Complimentary child care for hotel and casino guests. The childcare facility offers a variety of activities, including movies, games, crafts, puppet theater, and painting. Open 9:30 a.m. to 12:30 a.m., seven days a week. Parent or guardian must remain on property while the child is in the childcare center. Ages two through eight and potty trained. Limit four hours per day.

Orleans Hotel and Casino Kid's Tyme Child Care Center
702/365-7111

Open seven days a week for children three months to 12 years. The center features a jungle gym, movie room, arts and crafts, interactive play, and more. Open Sunday through Thursday, 9 a.m. to midnight, and Friday and Saturday, 9 a.m. to 1 a.m.

Kids Quest
www.kidsquest.com

This child-care franchise has locations at the Palms, Sunset Station, Boulder Station, and Texas Station. Supervised play area for children from six months to 12 years old. Maximum stay of 3½ hours and reservations are required for children 2 years old and younger. Hours are weekdays, 9 a.m. to 11 p.m., and weekends, 9 a.m. to 1 a.m. Call the individual hotels for more information or visit the Web site above.

Southern Nevada and Surrounding Area

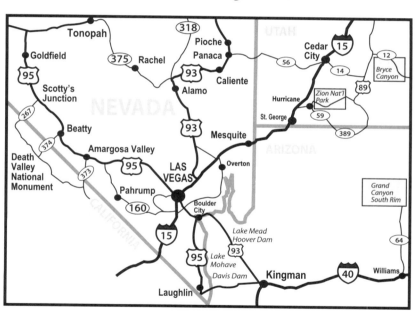

Las Vegas Strip

Downtown Las Vegas

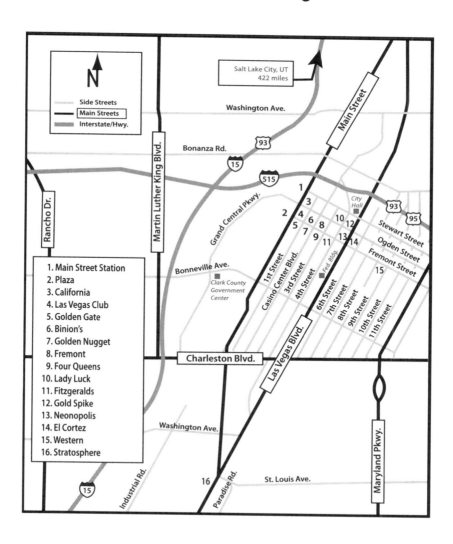

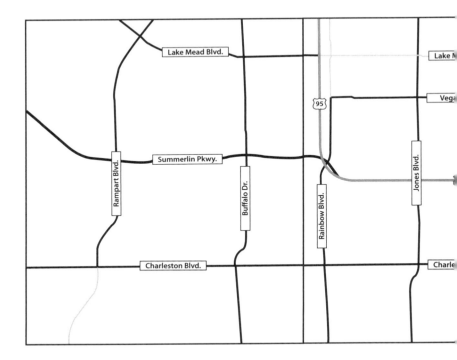

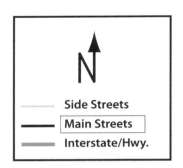

Side Streets
Main Streets
Interstate/Hwy.

Las Vegas Street Map

Index

About the Author

Kathy Espin is a freelance writer and public relations consultant who has lived in Las Vegas for 30 years. A former journalist, she spent 15 years in public relations, advertising, and marketing in the casino industry. She teaches public speaking, interpersonal communication, and public relations at the University of Nevada, Las Vegas, where she was named Part-Time Instructor of the Year in 2003. She volunteers her time as a Court-Appointed Special Advocate for foster children with the Clark County Juvenile Court. She is the mother of three grown children and has three granddaughters.

About Huntington Press

Huntington Press is a specialty publisher of Las Vegas- and gambling-related books and periodicals. Contact:

Huntington Press
3687 South Procyon Avenue
Las Vegas, Nevada 89103
702/252-0655
www.huntingtonpress.com

Hiking Las Vegas—60 Hikes Within 60 Minutes of the Strip
by Branch Whitney • Softcover • 269 pages • $17.95

If you're looking for something other than gambling, or for a Las Vegas vacation that leaves your body better off than your wallet, there's good news. Some of the best hiking, rock-scrambling, and bouldering trails in the country are within an hour's drive of the Las Vegas Strip.

Hiking Las Vegas details 40 hikes in the Red Rock Canyon Conservation Area and 20 hikes at Mt. Charleston. Whether you're a novice looking for a new adventure or an experienced hiker ready to test your skills, you'll find all the challenge you can handle in *Hiking Las Vegas*.

Hiking Southern Nevada—50 New Hikes
by Branch Whitney • Softcover • 213 pages • $17.95

In *Hiking Southern Nevada,* Branch Whitney details 50 new adventures-on-foot within an hour's drive of the bright lights of Las Vegas. Step-by-step directions, easy-to-follow maps, and quick-reference features guide you along the best trails in the area. From the multicolored sandstone of Red Rock Canyon and Valley of Fire to the crisp air and serenity of Mt. Charleston and the hot springs of Lake Mead, *Hiking Southern Nevada* is indispensable for anyone who wants to experience this magnificent corner of the Southwest.

Reservations Required —Culinary Secrets of Las Vegas' Celebrity Chefs
by Sarah Lee Marks • Softcover • 161 pages • $24.95

Wouldn't it be great if you could prepare a ribeye the way they do at N9NE? How about Picasso's warm lobster salad or Le Cirque's black truffle chicken? You can! These are just three of the 52 favorite recipes from the great restaurants and celebrity chefs of Las Vegas compiled in *Reservations Required*. Equal parts cookbook and guide to the city's best restaurants, *Reservations Required* will help you recreate and relive fabulous dining memories as you prepare these meals in your own kitchen. If you can't dine in every top restaurant in Las Vegas, you can still take a little bite of them home with you.

Neon Nuptials—The Complete Guide to Las Vegas Weddings
by Ken Van Vechten • Softcover • 240 pages • $14.95

Neon Nuptials is a no-holds-barred, independent, critical, and fun look at how and where to get married in Las Vegas. It visits each and every chapel—with a few stops at other less typical venues—and tells anticipatory brides (and at least a few grooms) exactly what's in store. You'll know everything there is to know about the beautiful, the bad, the kitschy, and even the touching in chapeldom. Yet *Neon Nuptials* is more than a Vegas wedding primer; it's also a guidebook that will add to the travel experience of even the most frequent Sin City visitor, with sure-fire bets on where to stay and eat, as well as what to see and do.